Psychological Effects
of
COCAINE
and
CRACK
Addiction

- **Anorexia Nervosa:**
  Starving for Attention

- **Child Abuse and Neglect:**
  Examining the Psychological Components

- **Conduct Unbecoming:**
  Hyperactivity, Attention Deficit, and Disruptive Behavior Disorders

- **Cutting the Pain Away:**
  Understanding Self-Mutilation

- **Drowning Our Sorrows:**
  Psychological Effects of Alcohol Abuse

- **Life Out of Focus:**
  Alzheimer's Disease and Related Disorders

- **The Mental Effects of Heroin**

- **Psychological Disorders Related to Designer Drugs**

- **Psychological Effects of Cocaine and Crack Addiction**

- **Schizophrenia:**
  Losing Touch with Reality

- **Sibling Rivalry:**
  Relational Disorders Between Brothers and Sisters

- **Smoke Screen:**
  Psychological Disorders Related to Nicotine Use

- **Through a Glass Darkly:**
  The Psychological Effects of Marijuana and Hashish

- **The Tortured Mind:**
  The Many Faces of Manic Depression

- **When Families Fail:**
  Psychological Disorders Caused by Parent-Child Relational Problems

- **A World Upside Down and Backwards:**
  Reading and Learning Disorders

Senior Consulting Editor Carol C. Nadelson, M.D.
Consulting Editor Claire E. Reinburg

Psychological Effects
of
COCAINE
and CRACK
Addiction

Ann Holmes

CHELSEA HOUSE PUBLISHERS
Philadelphia

The ENCYCLOPEDIA OF PSYCHOLOGICAL DISORDERS provides up-to-date information on the history of, causes and effects of, and treatment and therapies for problems affecting the human mind. The titles in this series are not intended to take the place of the professional advice of a psychiatrist or mental health care professional.

Chelsea House Publishers
Editor in Chief: Stephen Reginald
Managing Editor: James D. Gallagher
Production Manager: Pamela Loos
Art Director: Sara Davis
Director of Photography: Judy L. Hasday
Senior Production Editor: Lisa Chippendale

Staff for PSYCHOLOGICAL EFFECTS OF COCAINE AND CRACK ADDICTION
Editorial Assistant: Lily Sprague, Heather Forkos
Picture Researcher: Sandy Jones
Associate Art Director: Takeshi Takahashi
Designer: 21st Century Publishing and Communications, Inc.
Cover Design: Brian Wible

The ChelseaHouse World Wide Web site address is
http://www.chelseahouse.com

First Printing

9 8 7 6 5 4 3 2 1

Library of Congress Cataloging-in-Publication Data

Holmes, Ann (Ann E.)
Effects of cocaine and crack addiction / by Ann Holmes.
  p. cm.— (Encyclopedia of psychological disorders)
Includes bibliographical references and index.
Summary: Examines the problems associated with the use of crack and other forms of cocaine, focusing on the mental and psychological disorders that can occur.
ISBN 0-7910-4898-5
1. Crack (Drug)—Psychological aspects—Juvenile literature.
2. Crack (Drug)—Psychological effect—Juvenile literature.
3. Cocaine—Physiological aspects—Juvenile literature. 4. Cocaine—
Psychological effect—Juvenile literature.   [1. Crack (Drug)
2. Cocaine. 3. Drug abuse.]   I. Title.   II. Series.
HV5810.H65   1999
362.29'8—dc21   98-30975
                                                            CIP
                                                            AC

CONTENTS

PSYCHOLOGICAL DISORDERS AND THEIR EFFECT

CAROL C. NADELSON, M.D.
PRESIDENT AND CHIEF EXECUTIVE OFFICER,
The American Psychiatric Press

There are a wide range of problems that are considered psychological disorders, including mental and emotional disorders, problems related to alcohol and drug abuse, and some diseases that cause both emotional and physical symptoms. Psychological disorders often begin in early childhood, but during adolescence we see a sharp increase in the number of people affected by these disorders. It has been estimated that about 20 percent of the U.S. population will have some form of mental disorder sometime during their lifetime. Some psychological disorders appear following severe stress or trauma. Others appear to occur more often in some families and may have a genetic or inherited component. Still other disorders do not seem to be connected to any cause we can yet identify. There has been a great deal of attention paid to learning about the causes and treatments of these disorders, and exciting new research has taught us a great deal in the last few decades.

The fact that many new and successful treatments are available makes it especially important that we reject old prejudices and outmoded ideas that consider mental disorders to be untreatable. If psychological problems are identified early, it is possible to prevent serious consequences. We should not keep these problems hidden or feel shame that we or a member of our family has a mental disorder. Some people believe that something they said or did caused a mental disorder. Some people think that these disorders are "only in your head" so that you could "snap out of it" if you made the effort. This type of thinking implies that a treatment is a matter of willpower or motivation. It is a terrible burden for someone who is suffering to be blamed for their misery, and often people with psychological disorders are not treated compassionately. We hope that the information in this book will teach you about various mental illnesses.

The problems covered in the volumes in the ENCYCLOPEDIA OF PSYCHOLOGICAL DISORDERS were selected because they are of particular importance to young adults, because they affect them directly or because they affect family and friends. There are individual volumes on reading disorders, attention deficit and disruptive behavior disorders, and dementia—all of these are related to our abilities to learn and integrate information from the world around us. There are books on drug abuse that provide useful information about the effects of these drugs and treatments that are available for those individuals who have drug problems. Some of the books concentrate on one of the most common mental disorders, depression. Others deal with eating disorders, which are dangerous illnesses that affect a large number of young adults, especially women.

Most of the public attention paid to these disorders arises from a particular incident involving a celebrity that awakens us to our own vulnerability to psychological problems. These incidents of celebrities or public figures revealing their own psychological problems can also enable us to think about what we can do to prevent and treat these types of problems.

CRACK AND COCAINE: AN OVERVIEW

"Cocaine is the single most addicting drug known to mankind," says Alan I. Leshner, director of the National Institute on Drug Abuse (NIDA). "Mothers have given up their babies to get it." Not only have mothers surrendered their babies for money to buy drugs, people across all lines of race, gender, and economic status have given up their money, their mental well-being, their physical health, even their lives to feed an addiction to cocaine or crack.

No one is immune. Even those whose lives seem to be perfect can fall victim to the trap of cocaine and crack abuse. A chilling example was 22-year-old University of Maryland All-American basketball player Len Bias. The day after being selected in the first round of the 1986 National Basketball Association (NBA) draft by the Boston Celtics, a dream come true for any college basketball player, Bias died of a cocaine overdose in his college dorm room.

Crack and cocaine addict so many different types of people because they are easy to get, produce an almost immediate sense of well-being, and are relatively inexpensive. But the drugs' effects are a threat that does not just affect the individual user. In a 1994 study done by the NIDA, the number of pregnant women using crack, marijuana, heroin, or a psychedelic drug was estimated at 221,000. Of that group, an estimated 45,000 inhaled or injected cocaine and 35,000 smoked crack. These crack babies are often born premature, and the cost of hospital care for the babies can range from $2,500 to $5,000 per day.

With so many sad examples and staggering statistics of the widespread abuse of crack and cocaine, many people wonder how the problem will ever be solved. But strides are being made every day to teach children and adults about the dangers of these deadly drugs. This volume in THE ENCYCLOPEDIA OF PSYCHOLOGICAL DISORDERS takes an in-depth look at the history of cocaine and crack, the effects of these drugs, and current treatments and therapies that are being implemented in order to improve the lives of users as well as those of their family and friends.

Actor and comedian Chris Farley shortly before his death in 1997. Farley struggled with drug and alcohol problems for several years before he died of a cocaine overdose at age 33.

1

A DESTROYER OF LIVES

What do comedian Chris Farley, athlete Len Bias, and actor Robert Downey Jr. have in common? Each one's life has been changed, tragically, by cocaine, one of the most popular, controversial—and deadly—drugs.

■   ■   ■

Chris Farley deeply admired the late comedian John Belushi and was often called "the next Belushi" by fans. The two comedians had much in common. Both performed with Chicago's Second City improvisational comedy troupe and went on to stardom on *Saturday Night Live* (*SNL*). Many felt that Farley's off-the-wall, energetic physical comedy was reminiscent of Belushi's style. But Farley followed in his hero's footsteps in more than one way. Like Belushi, Chris Farley died suddenly and tragically at age 33 from a cocaine overdose when his career was starting to peak.

Farley joined *SNL* during the 1990–91 season and quickly became an audience favorite. The audience could always count on him for a wild, hilarious performance. One skit featured the bulky comedian as an overzealous, bare-chested dancer auditioning for the Chippendales. Other popular roles included one of a group of overweight and extremely devoted Chicago sports fans called the "Superfans," and the character of Matt Foley, an inept, loudmouthed motivational speaker.

Though Farley was clearly on the road to success, others at *SNL* were concerned about his health. Relatively short at 5 feet 8 inches in height, he was dangerously overweight at nearly 300 pounds. His struggles with cocaine and heroin addiction frightened friends the most; former *SNL* writer Al Franken told the *Chicago Tribune* that Lorne Michaels, the show's producer, had twice suspended Farley from the show and advised him to seek help for his drug and alcohol problems.

Farley left the cast of *SNL* after the 1994–95 season to concentrate on a career in films. After small roles in *Wayne's World, Wayne's World 2, Coneheads,* and *Billy Madison* (all movies starring fellow *SNL* alumni), Farley teamed up with *Saturday Night Live's* David Spade to play the lead role in *Tommy Boy.* The movie exceeded expectations at the box office and propelled Farley to stardom. He and Spade made a second comedy together, *Black Sheep,* which was also a financial success. He starred in the movie *Beverly Hills Ninja* and had completed filming the movie *Almost Heroes* when his longtime abuse of cocaine and heroin finally caught up with him. Farley's brother discovered his body on the floor of his apartment on the afternoon of December 18, 1997.

Farley had spent part of the summer of 1997 in rehabilitation but apparently resumed using cocaine and heroin in the weeks before his death. He appeared to have died of a heart attack. A few weeks later, the autopsy confirmed what many had suspected: the death had been caused by a drug overdose. Tests found cocaine and morphine in Farley's blood; atherosclerosis, or hardening of the arteries related to his drug abuse, had also contributed to his death.

Farley, who had admired John Belushi's career, had been unable to learn from Belushi's death from a cocaine overdose at age 33, and had shared his fate.

■   ■   ■

Basketball star Len Bias was a positive example to everyone who knew him. Neighbors described him as "an all-American kid," and "a local hero." On June 18, 1986, his dreams came true when he was chosen second overall and first by the Boston Celtics in the NBA draft. The dream ended the next day, when Len Bias was found dead of a cocaine overdose at the age of 22.

On the eve of the 1986 NBA draft, Bias seemed to symbolize the best a person could aspire to be. As a child, he had been a poor athlete—the one nobody wanted on his team, one of his earliest coaches recalled. But in countless workouts and games of one-on-one he competed fiercely, honing his talents and forcing his competitors to do the same.

Though he rose to stardom playing basketball, he never left the Maryland community where he was raised. He attended the University of Maryland, near his family's home, where he was an All-American

Friends of Len Bias carry his casket during a funeral procession for the 22-year-old basketball player. Bias overdosed on cocaine the night after he was drafted to play for the Boston Celtics.

player, but he often returned to the recreation center where he had played basketball as a child for weekly "Men's Night" games. Children would cluster around him, the star basketball player with the friendly grin, and he would remind them to study hard as well as play hard.

Bias flew home from Boston the night of the draft and arrived at his dorm around 11:30 P.M. At about 2:15 A.M. he left the dorm by himself for about an hour. Keeta Covington, a defensive back on the Maryland football team, walked Bias out to his car. Later he told reporters that Bias was tired of all of the questions surrounding the draft and needed to get away from everything for a while. One of his friends reported seeing him at a small off-campus party during the interval he was away.

Bias was reportedly sitting on a couch in his dormitory suite in Washington Hall talking with teammate Terry Long when he collapsed some time after 6 A.M. Long unsuccessfully administered cardiopulmonary resuscitation until paramedics arrived and rushed Bias to the hospital. For two hours, emergency room staff members tried to revive him, but their efforts proved unsuccessful.

The death was a national shock. Cocaine had ended Bias's dream-come-true life before his NBA career had even begun. The community that had revered and admired Len Bias was now forced to look upon him as a tragic example rather than a heroic one.

■　　　　■　　　　■

Oscar-nominated actor Robert Downey Jr. has appeared in many successful movies and is considered one of the most talented young actors of his generation. In the past few years, however, Downey's problems with cocaine and other drugs have attracted as much attention as his films.

Downey has attempted to end his drug habit several times—without success. "Stopping isn't hard," he once remarked. "Not starting again is." In 1996 he was arrested three times within 30 days on drug-related charges. On June 23, 1996, police pulled Downey Jr. over for speeding and discovered cocaine, heroin, and an unloaded .357 Magnum in the back of his pickup truck. Police arrested him in early July after he allegedly entered a neighbor's home in Malibu, California, where he was discovered asleep in a child's bed. He was arrested a third time for leaving a drug-treatment center, where he had been placed by court order. In November 1996 Downey was sentenced to three years' probation and placed under 24-hour surveillance at the Exodus Recovery Center.

Actor Sean Penn is among many friends who tried to convince Robert Downey Jr. to get himself help. Downey recalled, "I remember [Penn] saying 'You have two reputations, and I think you'd do well to get rid of one of those reputations. If you don't, it will get rid of the other one.'" His friend's advice went unheeded, and in December 1997 Robert Downey Jr. was found in possession of cocaine and heroin. This violated his parole, and he was sentenced to six months in prison. On March 31, 1998, he was released from Los Angeles County Jail to enter a drug-treatment center, still battling his addiction to cocaine. There is no doubt that a cloud will continue to hang over his career until he puts drugs behind him forever.

Actor Robert Downey Jr., whose career has been jeopardized multiple times because of his cocaine abuse, has found it very hard to quit the drug despite his legal troubles and his friends' concern for him.

WHAT ARE COCAINE AND CRACK?

Cocaine comes from the coca plant, *Erythroxylon coca*, which grows mainly in the Andes Mountains of South America. The coca plant's effects can be felt in a number of ways: by ingesting coca leaves, smoking coca paste, inhaling or injecting cocaine hydrochloride, or smoking "freebase" cocaine. Although these forms differ in strength due to different levels of purity, cocaine is the active ingredient—the one that produces the desired reaction—in each preparation.

The leaves of the coca plant can be chewed, although this method is generally limited to native populations in South America. It is estimated that as many as 90 percent of the mountain population still chew the leaves in order to combat fatigue and hunger. The effects of the coca leaves last only for an hour or two, so the Peruvian natives carry the leaves in their cheeks so that low levels of cocaine are released into their systems throughout the day. South American natives also make a paste, called *basulca*, with the coca leaves that can be smoked.

Cocaine hydrochloride powder is the form most frequently found in the United States. This white powder has a salty or slightly bitter taste that numbs the tongue and lips. It is usually inhaled through the nostrils ("snorting") or dissolved in water and injected into the body with a hypodermic needle. Cocaine powder is prepared by placing coca leaves in a press with sulfuric acid, kerosene, or gasoline and crushing the mixture. This creates a mash that is 40 to 90 percent cocaine sulfate. To remove impurities, this mash is treated with hydrochloric acid, which produces the white powder. If the hydrochloride portion of this compound is removed by heating it with a volatile solvent such as ether or ammonia (this process is known as "freebasing,") the resulting cocaine base can be smoked.

Another commonly used form of cocaine in the United States is "crack," a cocaine alkaloid that is formed by mixing coca mash, hydrochloride salt, and baking soda, and allowing this combination to dry into chunks, called "rocks." Crack looks like small lumps of soap but feels hard and smooth, like porcelain. Like freebase cocaine, crack is smoked and its effects hit quickly.

Like every illegal drug, cocaine has a variety of street names: "coke," "C," "snow," "flakes," "sugar," "blow," "toot," "nose candy," and "The Lady." Crack is sometimes called "rock" or "readyrock." In some areas, it is sold in three-inch sticks with ridges that are called "french fries" or "teeth."

Cocaine is usually shipped from South America in two forms: rock cocaine, which looks like pebbles and is about 70 percent pure, and flake cocaine, which is more refined and can be 100 percent pure. However, in the United States, drug dealers often "cut" the cocaine, or dilute it with inactive ingredients, to stretch their supply. Ingredients commonly added to the drug include sugar, flour, talc, and baking soda. If cocaine is cut so much that it loses its effect, other active ingredients, like caffeine or amphetamines, can be added. Cocaine sold on the street can be as little as 12 to 15 percent pure. The added impurities increase the danger of taking cocaine,

Cocaine is most often used in powder form in the United States; it is typically inhaled, or "snorted," although sometimes it is dissolved in water and injected.

because they may cause unexpected side effects and users have no idea how much of the drug they're actually taking.

Cocaine is also used in combination with many different illegal drugs. These include heroin (this combination is called "dynamite," "goofball," or "speedball"), heroin and LSD ("Frisco special" or "Frisco speedball"), morphine ("C & M"), and various other combinations ("cotton brothers" is a mix of cocaine, heroin and morphine). Crack and phencyclidine (PCP) combined is called "beam me up scottie," "space cadet," or "tragic magic." Because these drugs often have different effects, combining them can overload a person's system, with deadly results.

These photos of a U.S. customs official, above, with a shipment of 132 pounds of cocaine concealed in Valentine's Day roses from Colombia, and a Hong Kong customs agent with a shipment of 23.5 pounds of heroin hidden in film canisters, show the variety of ways drug dealers attempt to smuggle their cargo across international boundaries.

PABLO ESCOBAR AND
THE COLOMBIAN CARTELS

On December 2, 1993, Colombian soldiers shot and killed Pablo Escobar, the fugitive leader of a multibillion-dollar international criminal organization based in Medellín, Colombia. Under Escobar's leadership, the cartel had funneled tons of cocaine into the United States, virtually controlling the flow of the drug into cities like New York and Miami. A rival cartel, based in Cali, Colombia, had tried to undercut the Medellín cartel's prices on cocaine and destroy its market by competition, but it was the antidrug effort by Colombian government officials in the late 1980s and early 1990s that brought the Medellín cartel down. Police and military initiatives increased after the cartel brought more violence and terrorism to the country, funneling money and supplies to leftist guerrillas. Escobar's underlings, "lieutenants" in the cartel, began to be arrested or killed by police, and some of them turned informer, testifying to help police track down other drug traffickers. Finally, in late 1991, Escobar was captured and held in a luxury prison built specially for him as a part of his surrender deal.

Escobar continued to run his drug operations from prison, however, and in July of 1992 he escaped. A fugitive, he directed the course of the cartel's business as he moved from one "safe house" to another, though the cartel was beginning to fall apart: more of his lieutenants surrendered or were captured, and others defected to the rival Cali cartel. Finally, at the end of 1993, Escobar made the mistake of calling a radio station to protest the fact that officials would not let his family leave the country, and police managed to trace the call to a house in Medellín. They surrounded the house, and Escobar was killed as he and his bodyguards attempted to escape.

Unfortunately, the destruction of the Medellín cartel and the demise of its leader did not disrupt the flow of cocaine out of Colombia. The Cali cartel, which had battled for supremacy in the market for eight years, now found itself without competition and increased its production and smuggling of cocaine. Six months after Escobar's death, cocaine smuggling into the United States remained at the same level, with prices and supply still constant. The flow of cocaine and heroin into Europe had even increased. Despite the efforts of U.S. officials, the activities of the Cali cartel have been difficult to curb.

HOW COCAINE GETS TO THE UNITED STATES

Most of the world's cocaine supply is processed in South America. The coca plant is cultivated in the mountain valleys of Peru, Bolivia, Colombia, Ecuador, and Brazil and processed in laboratories, especially in Colombia. For many rural farmers, the cocaine industry is their only reliable source of income. In Peru, Bolivia, and Colombia, for example, an estimated one million farmers grow coca plants and process and export cocaine products. In Peru, as many as 60,000 families are thought to depend solely on growing coca plants to survive, and in Bolivia, approximately 5 to 6 percent of the population is directly involved in the cocaine industry.

Usually the coca leaves are made into paste in Bolivia or Peru, then smuggled to Colombia either overland in cars, trucks, or buses, by ship along the Pacific coast, or in boats on the Amazon River. In large Colombian cities like Medellín, Cali, and Bogotá, the paste is processed in laboratories into cocaine powder, which is easier to hide and transport. From Colombia, the drug is smuggled into the United States. Popular entry points are Florida, and Texas and California via the Mexican border.

Cocaine is brought into the United States by land, sea, and air. It has been brought into the country hidden in many items, from teddy bears to handicrafts to golf cart tires to boxes of snacks. In other cases, drug smugglers, or "couriers," have had packets of cocaine surgically implanted under the skin of their thighs or have swallowed balloons filled with the drug, which can later be purged from the system. This method has been deadly on more than one occasion; if the balloon bursts while in the courier's stomach, the large amount of cocaine it contains poisons him or her almost instantly.

"Rocks" of crack cocaine are made by combining powder cocaine with baking soda, water, and a special chemical, then boiling the mixture. Crack cocaine became instantly popular when it hit the markets in the mid-1980s because it was relatively inexpensive and offered a fast, intense high.

2

HISTORY OF COCAINE USE

The coca plant, from which cocaine is derived, has been grown and culti-vated in Central and South America for thousands of years. The Incas and other native cultures either chewed the coca leaves or used them to brew a form of tea in order to receive the plant's stimulating effects.

Researchers have discovered that coca leaves have significant amounts of calcium, iron, phosphorus, and vitamins B_2, A, and E. Because it can be difficult to grow food in the higher elevations of South America, coca leaves may have been used in the past as much for their nutritional value as for their stimulant effects. The use of coca leaves reduced the Indians' desire for food and increased their ability to work strenuously at high alti-tudes. Coca leaves were also easier to carry than bulky food and were used by Native American runners on long-distance journeys.

The Andes Mountain Indians also used coca to treat a number of medical problems, including muscle pain, rheumatism, asthma, and stomach ulcers. A paste made from the leaves was used to treat skin sores, headaches, and gum disease.

Despite its widespread use in South America, little attention was paid to coca by Europeans and North Americans until cocaine was isolated as its active ingredient by German scientist Albert Niemann in 1860. Twenty-four years later, New York surgeon William Stewart Halsted injected a patient with cocaine, pioneering the practice of local anesthesia. That same year, 1884, a New York ophthalmologist, Carl Killer, introduced cocaine as a local anesthetic during eye surgery. Cocaine was especially effective for use during surgery because it caused blood vessels to shrink, limiting bleeding. Doctors also found that cocaine blocked nerve signals to the brain, and they began to use it widely as an anesthetic (in fact, the only legal use of cocaine in the United States today is as a local anesthetic for surgery). Cocaine was also prescribed as a cure for alcohol and morphine

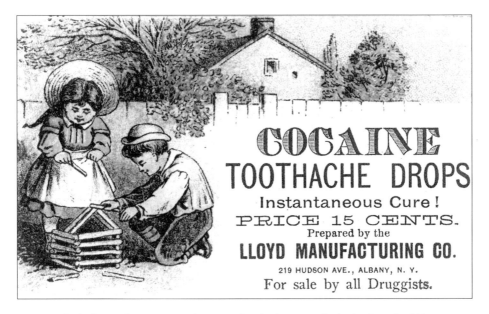

In the late 19th century, cocaine was advertised as a medical miracle and sold in many products. Here, cocaine's anesthetic properties make it the crucial ingredient in a toothache "cure."

addiction—ironic, given its own addictive qualities, which had not yet been discovered.

In the 1880s the "father of psychoanalysis," Sigmund Freud, began to experiment with cocaine, testing the drug's physical and psychological effects. His research, which is mainly contained in the book *Über Coca*, led Freud to believe that cocaine was a "miracle drug" capable of curing a variety of ailments and making life more pleasant. In *Über Coca* he suggested that cocaine be used to cure depression, to increase a person's physical capacity during stressful times, and to restore mental capacity decreased by fatigue. He also recommended cocaine to help digestive disorders of the stomach, asthma, and skin diseases.

In part because of Freud's influential writings, use of the drug spread. By 1890 cocaine was being added to thousands of tonics and other "patent medicines" that claimed to cure illnesses ranging from tuberculosis to impotence, asthma, alcoholism, and the common cold. These claims were all shown later to be false. Cocaine was also added to non-medical products, including wine, soda pop (cocaine was an original ingredient in Coca-Cola, hence its name), nasal sprays, gum, cigars, cigarettes, and suppositories. Because manufacturers were not required to label their products with an ingredient list, most customers never knew what they were consuming. To correct this, Congress passed the Pure Food and Drug Act of 1906, requiring that ingredients be listed on labels. Because of new reports on the danger of cocaine addiction—including essays from Freud, whose close friend had died as a result of cocaine after he prescribed it to treat his morphine addiction—demand for products with cocaine virtually disappeared.

By 1914 concern over the addictive qualities and negative effects of cocaine use caused it to be banned by the Harrison Narcotics Act, the first federal antidrug law. Since that time, recreational use of cocaine has been illegal, and the manufacture and distribution of the drug for medical purposes is strictly regulated.

COCAINE BECOMES POPULAR

From the passage of the Harrison Act until the late 1960s, very few people used cocaine for recreational purposes. Those who did use it were usually entertainers, who liked the lift the drug gave them. Because there were so few cocaine users, and because few of them ever exhibited problems or entered therapy for addiction, a perception grew that cocaine was a "safe" drug.

In the early 1970s, cocaine began to come into fashion. The growing nightclub culture, which glamorized a fast-paced lifestyle and material excess, embraced the drug, causing it to become extremely popular in discotheques. The high price of cocaine made it a status symbol, a way to show off the high degree of financial success necessary to afford a cocaine habit. (To sustain a serious cocaine habit required several thousand dollars per week—thereby drastically limiting the number of people who could indulge in the drug.) The falsely inflated sense of self-esteem that the drug produced also appealed to this flashy, extravagant lifestyle; people using cocaine felt like the world revolved around them. The image of a fashionable club-goer snorting cocaine off a mirror with a rolled-up $100 bill, or wearing a small gold spoon on a chain around his or her neck, became an emblem of the decadence of the culture of discotheques and nightclubs. This trend of increasing use continued into the beginning of the 1980s, as cocaine began to be viewed as a "power drug" that executives and Wall Street brokers used, a symbol of success and drive and the high-energy life that cocaine seemed to encourage.

In the early 1980s when the cost of the drug dropped and it became more available, cocaine use reached epidemic proportions. Between 1974 and 1982, the number of people who had tried cocaine once jumped from 5.4 million to 21.6 million. Between 1977 and 1979, the number of regular cocaine users (defined as using the drug at least once a month) increased from 1.6 million to 4.3 million. By 1985, according to government statistics, that number was 5.7 million regular cocaine users.

Although the increase in cocaine use started among more affluent individuals during the 1970s, the appearance of a new form, crack, has shifted the user demographics to include lower socioeconomic groups living in large metropolitan areas. In the 1980s cocaine also started to become a problem in rural areas that previously had been spared the difficulties associated with such rampant illicit drug use.

A NEW DRUG APPEARS: CRACK

While traditionally the most popular way to take cocaine is by "snorting," or inhaling the powder, in the early 1980s a way to smoke the drug, known as "freebasing," started to become popular. To free-base, the cocaine is mixed with baking soda, ammonium hydroxide, and water, then combined with a fast-drying solvent such as ether. This leaves a hard crystalline base that can be smoked in a water pipe or added to a nicotine or marijuana cigarette.

Freebasing delivers a more intense high than snorting cocaine, but the process is time-consuming and can be dangerous. Ether is highly flammable and can explode. In 1985 it was reported that popular comedian Richard Pryor was badly burned in such an explosion when he was freebasing cocaine. Years later, however, Pryor admitted that there had not been an explosion; actually, he had become depressed after heavy cocaine use and had deliberately set himself on fire.

As a result of the possibility of explosions, there was a demand for a ready-to-smoke type of cocaine, and New York City drug dealers came up with a new drug: crack. Crack is prepared by combining cocaine with a special chemical similar to the anesthetic drug lidocaine (and nicknamed "comeback" by dealers), baking soda, and water; bringing the mixture to a boil or putting it in a microwave; then allowing it to

Comedian Richard Pryor talks with Barbara Walters in an interview one month after he was badly burned, reportedly by an explosion while he was preparing to freebase cocaine. The ether involved in freebasing is highly flammable, and explosions of this type kept freebasing from becoming more popular. Years later, Pryor admitted that there had not been an explosion; rather, he had become so depressed after long-term cocaine use that he had set himself on fire.

cool into a solid mass. This is broken into smaller chunks, called "rocks," which can be smoked in a glass pipe.

Dealers took quickly to the new drug. Because making crack involved combining cocaine with other chemicals—in effect, "cutting"

COCAINE AND POPULAR CULTURE

Cocaine has long had a hold on the imagination, and this is reflected in music lyrics, literature, and movies. In the 1980s, cocaine's rise in popularity—as well as the drug's devastating effects on the user—was highlighted in books such as Jay McInerney's *Bright Lights, Big City*, the story of a young man who loses his wife, his job, and nearly his soul because of cocaine.

One of the heroes of classic detective fiction is intellectual, distinguished in appearance—and a habitual cocaine user. Sir Arthur Conan Doyle's character Sherlock Holmes—with his trademark deerstalker hat, caped coat, and pipe—was one of the earliest and most memorable detectives in modern Western fiction. Holmes's "elementary" deductions always amazed his partner, John Watson, a physician. Watson often expressed concern about his friend's cocaine habit. Although many movies about the exploits and adventures of Sherlock Holmes have been made over the years, *The Seven Percent Solution*, released in 1976, is based on Watson's attempt to cure Holmes of his cocaine addiction.

The Seven Percent Solution was hardly the first film to deal with cocaine and drug abuse. As early as 1914, Hollywood was producing films addressing drug-related issues, beginning with the release of *Cocaine Traffic; Or, the Drug Terror*. This silent film was also known as *Drug Terror; Or, the Underworld Exposed*. A 1936 movie, *The Pace That Kills*, was also reissued in the United States as *Cocaine Fiends*. More recent films include *Cocaine Cowboys* (1979), featuring Jack Palance and Andy Warhol; the made-for-television movie *Cocaine—One Man's Seduction*, which appeared in 1983; and *True Romance*, a 1993 film in which newlyweds find a big stash of cocaine and attempt to sell it.

In one scene from the 1994 movie *Pulp Fiction*, a glamorous woman who is a drug dealer's girlfriend (played by Uma Thurman) finds a packet of white powder in the coat pocket of another character (played by John Travolta). Believing that the powder is cocaine, she snorts some of it. However, the drug she has just taken turns out to be extremely pure heroin, and she lapses into a coma-like state from the overdose, her eyes rolling back in her head and her lips turning blue. John Travolta's character gives graphic and rugged first aid by plunging a hypodermic needle into her chest as she convulses. "I don't know how anybody could sit through that scene and do another snort of cocaine," said David Horowitz of the Center for the Study of Popular Culture in Los Angeles. This graphic depiction of the consequences of drug abuse is a far cry from Woody Allen's sneezing away a line of cocaine in the 1977 film *Annie Hall*.

Many of the brightest stars of Hollywood have died because of cocaine, including actors River Phoenix and Chris Farley, comedian John Belushi, and producer Don Simpson. Actress/model Margeaux Hemingway, whose blond hair and striking dark eyebrows helped popularize the 1980s "natural look," was another prominent victim of cocaine. The granddaughter of legendary American writer Ernest Hemingway, she was also one of the highest paid models of the '80s. However, Margeaux was also a frequent guest of Studio 54, a trendy New York City nightclub notorious for its wild parties, celebrity clientele, and cocaine traffic. Alcohol and drug use eventually eroded her looks and her career, and she committed suicide—by a drug overdose—in 1996.

The careers of many others, such as Richard Pryor and Robert Downey Jr., have been affected by the drug. Even entertainers who do not use cocaine have found their lives impacted by its negative effects. Hugh O'Connor, the son of actor Carroll O'Connor (*All in the Family*, *In the Heat of the Night*), struggled with alcohol and drug dependency for many years. He shot himself in 1995 at age 32 during a cocaine binge. After Hugh's death, his celebrity father actively sought and brought to trial the dealer who sold his son his final, fatal, dose of cocaine. O'Connor remains an active antidrug campaigner. "The reality is that Hollywood universally has a very dim view of drugs and the consequences of drug taking," says Hollywood screenwriter Lionel Chetwynd.

Since the 1930s, popular music has addressed cocaine use. From the 1930s song "Cocaine Bill and Morphine Sue," to the Grateful Dead's 1960s anthem "Casey Jones" to Eric Clapton's "Cocaine," the drug has been both vilified and celebrated. Even heavy metal band Metallica wrote a song called "Master of Puppets" about cocaine's ability to control its users' lives, and the emptiness of its promises.

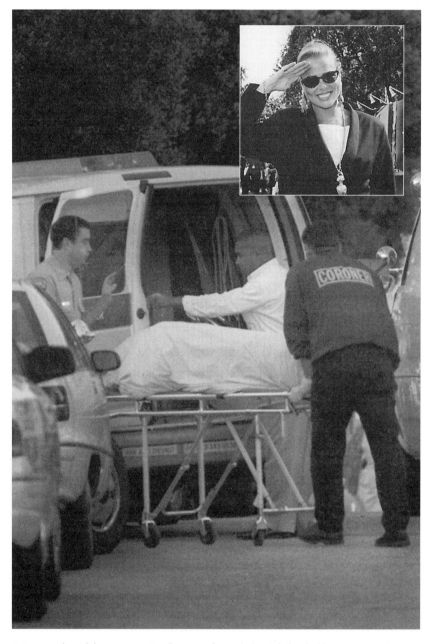

Actress and model Margeaux Hemingway, shown in inset, is loaded into a coroner's van after her body was discovered on July 1, 1996. Hemingway, the granddaughter of writer Ernest Hemingway, died of a cocaine overdose.

the cocaine instead of selling it at higher purity levels—while maintaining its effects, dealers could sell it at cheaper prices than powder cocaine, and thereby sell it to people who couldn't afford the more expensive high. At $3 to $5 per rock, crack was significantly cheaper than powder, and its use spread into the inner cities of America. The drug seemed to afford a quick, cheap, thrilling high, and thousands of inner-city residents started using crack, often without realizing how serious and immediate the potential for addiction—or death—was.

COCAINE AND CRACK USE TODAY

Thanks in large part to antidrug campaigns, use of all illicit drugs declined in the late 1980s. In 1996 an estimated 3.6 million Americans were regular cocaine users, down from 5.7 million in 1985, according to the Office of National Drug Control Policy. However, the drug is still one of the most popular in this country. Each year, the government estimates, over 300 tons of cocaine are smuggled into the country. Even more disturbing is that in each year since 1991, cocaine and crack use has risen.

According to the Office of National Drug Control Policy's winter 1997 report, *Pulse Check*, the market for cocaine and crack has stabilized. The report also noted, "While crack cocaine is still the dominant illicit drug on the national scene, it appears that crack users are an aging group. Some sources report that crack use has become unfashionable and has developed the image of a 'junkie' or 'burnout' drug among young, new drug users."

When cocaine is snorted, the user will typically begin to feel its effects within just a few minutes. However, the effects do not last long, and as they wear off the user may feel depressed, listless, or edgy.

3

HOW COCAINE AND CRACK WORK

What is it about cocaine and crack that is so attractive that people will inhale, smoke, or inject these highly addictive drugs? The main reason is that cocaine and crack elevate the user's mood, often within just a few minutes, and provide a sense of well-being, confidence, exhilaration, or ecstasy. The downside—from a user's point of view—is that the effects do not last long. As they wear off, depression and edginess set in. To maintain the euphoric feelings, the user needs to use the drug again or increase the amount used, leading to tolerance. Continued use of the substance in greater and greater amounts leads to addiction—the feeling that you can't function without the drug.

People take substances such as cocaine in order to change the way they feel: to reduce pain, to stimulate the body, to induce relaxation, or to produce feelings of intoxication. The most common effects of cocaine intoxication include:

- difficulties in perception (knowing what is or isn't real)
- wakefulness, or a feeling of alertness
- impairment to attention span and judgment
- disruptive behavior
- awkward physical movement.

Cocaine intoxication is different from the effects produced by alcohol or other drugs. The frequency of cocaine use, the amount of the drug taken, and even the user's expectation of how the drug will make him or her feel can affect the drug's intoxicating effects.

When a person cannot stop using a substance such as cocaine, alcohol, or heroin, we say he or she is addicted, or substance-dependent. A person who is addicted to cocaine will continue to abuse the drug despite the significant problems this causes. Addiction often combines both physical dependence and psychological dependence. Physical dependence means that the person's body has become so used to the drug that unpleasant physical symptoms will occur if it is withdrawn suddenly. Psychological dependence means that the drug user has a powerful craving to use the drug, even if there is no physical drive to do so. Different drugs combine these effects in different amounts. Heroin, for example, causes a high degree of physical dependence; nicotine, on the other hand, has low levels of physical dependence, but the psychological dependence can continue for years after the user quits.

Tolerance is a need for greater and greater amounts of the drug to achieve the intoxication, or "high." As a person uses cocaine he or she becomes tolerant of the drug's effects, and must take larger amounts to achieve the same "buzz," or euphoric feeling, that occurred when the user first started taking the drug. In time, many drug abusers develop such high tolerance for their drug that they can take an amount that would kill a nonuser. Many drug-related deaths occur when first-time users take a dose that is too high.

Withdrawal occurs when a person's body has become so used to a drug that it adapts chemically, becoming physically dependent on the drug. When that person stops taking the drug and amounts of the substance in the body decline, unpleasant symptoms occur. These can be both mental and physical and may include severe muscle cramps, nausea, convulsions, depression, irritability, and hallucinations. The symptoms of withdrawal can be so unpleasant that the user will continue to take the drug just to avoid them.

HOW COCAINE IS TAKEN

There are many ways that cocaine can enter a user's system. It can be ingested orally or taken intranasally (through the nose), intravenously, or by smoking the drug.

Chapter 2 noted that the natives living in the Andes Mountains of South America often chew the leaves of the coca plant for energy. Cocaine can easily be absorbed into a person's system orally, through the absorbent tissues of the mouth. To help the system absorb the drug, Peruvian Indians often combine powdered lime or ash with the coca leaves. The leaves are also brewed into a potent tea, and a paste made from the coca leaves is smoked by South American natives as well.

Actor River Phoenix died of a multiple-drug overdose at age 23. Along with abusing Valium and alcohol, Phoenix appeared to have injected a "speedball," an extremely dangerous mixture of cocaine and heroin.

In the United States, cocaine is most commonly snorted. The white powder is finely chopped, divided into thin rows or "lines," and inhaled through a tube. Sometimes short straws are used to snort the cocaine; in the extravagant drug culture of the 1970s and 1980s, $50 or $100 bills were often rolled into a tight straw. When cocaine is snorted, its effects begin to be felt within a few minutes, peak within 15 to 20 minutes, and begin to disappear within an hour.

Cocaine powder can also be melted and mixed with water, then injected into a vein. Injection produces a more powerful effect than snorting does, but using a needle greatly increases a user's health risks. Complications range from painful skin sores at the injection site to an increased risk of getting acquired immune deficiency syndrome (AIDS) or hepatitis from a shared needle. Because of these risks, and the social stigma attached to needle use (many users believe that someone who uses a needle must be seriously addicted, and may justify their own use by saying that using needles is worse), injecting cocaine is not nearly as popular a method as snorting.

Freebase cocaine and crack are always smoked. The high is more intense than that felt with snorting or injection, but the effects last only about 15 minutes.

Crack and cocaine are often used in conjunction with other drugs. The most common is alcohol, but marijuana and tranquilizers are often taken with or after cocaine use. Cocaine is sometimes mixed with heroin to make a "speedball," or with the hallucinogen PCP to make "space base." However, mixing cocaine and other drugs greatly increases the danger of abuse, or of an adverse reaction to the combination. Cocaine (a powerful stimulant) and heroin (a powerful depressant) is a particularly dangerous combination: popular comedian John Belushi died in 1982 after being injected with a speedball. He was 33 years old. Another celebrity, actor River Phoenix, was 23 when he died of a multiple-drug overdose outside a Hollywood nightclub in 1993. The autopsy showed that there were deadly levels of cocaine, heroin, alcohol, and Valium in his bloodstream when he died.

COCAINE'S EFFECT ON THE BRAIN AND NERVOUS SYSTEM

Cocaine acts as a powerful psychomotor stimulant (meaning it causes a person to feel energized and "sped up"), a strong local anesthetic (a drug that keeps someone from feeling pain in a specific area), and a vasoconstrictor (a drug that narrows, or constricts, the blood vessels). These effects are due to the way that cocaine blocks the normal functioning of the nervous system.

For a person to feel a sensation, such as pain, an electrical impulse must travel through the nervous system and up to the person's brain. To do so, the electrical impulse must be passed from one neuron to the next by a system using charged particles called ions to stimulate chemicals called neurotransmitters. If either the ions or the neurotransmitters are disrupted, the sensation will not reach the brain. When cocaine is used for its anesthetic properties, it inhibits the ions in the nervous system from moving along the neuron. Since the ions cannot trigger the action of the neurotransmitters, the next neuron in the chain does not receive the signal and cannot pass it on to the brain.

In both the brain and the nervous system, cocaine also acts to change the way the body handles its neurotransmitters. After they have been fired, the body has a mechanism to pump the neurotransmitter chemicals back into the nerve cells that released them. Cocaine blocks this mechanism from working on some neurotransmitters, especially norepinephrine (NE). Since the NE is not returned to the nerve cell, its stimulating effect on the receptors continues for a longer time.

Wherever NE acts as a neurotransmitter in the body, cocaine will have stimulating effects. This includes both the brain and spinal cord, or central nervous system, and the cardiovascular system. Because of its effects on the cardiovascular system, moderate doses of cocaine will cause a person's heart rate and blood pressure to increase. Higher doses of cocaine will produce more severe effects; at a high enough dose, cocaine will result in death by cardiac failure as the heart tries to pump too hard through blood vessels that are too constricted.

Cocaine is called a psychomotor stimulant because it affects several of the neurotransmitters in the brain, including NE, dopamine, and serotonin. In lab animals, low doses of cocaine or other stimulants enhance locomotion, grooming, and exploring behavior. At higher doses, these behaviors disappear and are replaced by repeated unvarying behavior, such as licking, gnawing, or sniffing. If the dose is increased further, convulsions, coma, or death may result.

The respiratory system is also affected by cocaine, and body temperature often rises. At high doses, humans also show tremors and convulsions, which can lead to the collapse of the central nervous system, causing respiratory and/or cardiac failure and thereby death.

Cocaine can immediately take over a user's life, setting that person up for a hard fall that can include lost jobs, broken families, jail time, or death.

The electrical activity of the brain has been observed to increase during cocaine intoxication. Activity is especially increased in the amygdala, which is the "pleasure center," and in the limbic system, which controls basic functions like movement, breathing, and heartbeat. After repeated exposure to cocaine, parts of the limbic system seem to become damaged, growing more susceptible to a type of seizure that closely resembles epilepsy. The changes in electrical activity caused by repeated cocaine use may also be the cause of the hypersensitivity and toxic psychosis that heavy users sometimes show.

Researchers also suspect that this change in brain electricity may cause changes in the brain's structure over time. This would explain why, even after years of abstinence, former cocaine addicts can feel extreme cravings.

WHY DO PEOPLE GET STARTED?

What factors influence a person to begin using drugs? First, peer pressure. Drug use by friends is consistently the strongest predictor of a young person's involvement with drugs. Drug use begins and continues largely because young people have contact with peers who use drugs and who provide the role models and social support for drug taking. Family influences are also important factors. Families with inconsistent discipline, drug-using parents, or distant relationships between parents and children may foster drug use. The structure of a family (single parent, two parents, etc.) is not as important as the closeness of the family members, especially the young person and parent(s). Young people who become involved with drugs are most often those whose parents a) have little control over their children and are unsupportive and b) place less value on traditional goals like obtaining an education or encouraging a work ethic.

Personality factors may play a role as well. Some studies suggest that rebelliousness, low self-esteem, alienation, and a high tolerance for social deviance may indicate a potential for drug use, and drug use can reflect an antisocial personality. Poor school performance can also lead to drug use among young people. However, there are many reasons people use drugs, and no specific set of circumstances is always connected with drug use.

Finally, cocaine is attractive because there is money in it, both in the United States and in the cocaine-producing countries abroad. With estimated annual revenues higher than $100 billion in the United States, cocaine is extremely popular with dealers, and many users turn to dealing to raise the money to support their own habit. And as was mentioned in the first chapter, in some of the economically depressed countries of South America the cocaine industry may be the only reliable source of income for rural people.

Regardless of the reasons, once drug use begins it can take immediate hold of a person's life. This is especially true of cocaine use, which impacts both the physical and psychological health of its user. In the following chapters, we'll examine how cocaine use affects a person's mental and physical health.

Injecting cocaine, or any other drug, can lead to collapsed veins or infections at the injection site, as well as more serious consequences such as contracting AIDS or hepatitis.

4

THE PHYSICAL EFFECTS OF CRACK AND COCAINE

Cocaine causes a wide variety of physical reactions in the user's body. These physical effects can include increased heart and breathing rates, increased blood pressure, nausea and vomiting, weight loss, tremors (or "shakes"), inability to sleep, twitching, fever, paleness, sexual impotence, dilated or enlarged pupils, cold sweats, fatigue, constipation, headaches, blurred vision, seizures, and nasal congestion. Over time, cocaine use can lead to ulceration of the nasal membranes, cardiac arrest, respiratory arrest, lung damage, and coma.

Some of the physical effects of cocaine are linked to the way the drug is taken. For example, persons who snort cocaine often do major damage to their noses. They develop sinusitis (irritation and bleeding of the nasal tissues) and a perforated, or torn, nasal septum (the thin tissue membrane between the nostrils). After a period of time, the lining of the nose can actually begin to dissolve. People who inject cocaine have puncture marks, or "tracks," most commonly on their forearms, similar to the ones seen in people who inject heroin. They also are at a high risk for contracting AIDS. Injecting drugs repeatedly into the same area can cause veins to collapse, and can lead to sores or ulcers developing in the skin from infections in the punctures.

Smoking cocaine or crack can cause chronic sore throat and hoarseness; shortness of breath; bronchitis; lung cancer; emphysema and other lung damage; and respiratory problems like congestion, wheezing, and coughing up black phlegm or mucus. Lung infections such as tuberculosis become more common as the lungs grow more damaged from habitual use. Crack use can also result in other physical problems, including burns on the lips, tongue, and throat; slowed digestion; weight loss; increased blood pressure and heart rate; brain seizures; lack of desire for food and sex; dilated pupils; and in severe cases, heart attacks and stroke.

Cocaine dependence (with any method of administration) is commonly associated with signs of weight loss and malnutrition, such as anemia, brittle bones, and bleeding gums, because of its appetite-suppressing effects. Addicts may also suffer from chronic insomnia from the constant presence of such a strong stimulant.

PHYSICAL DAMAGE CAUSED BY THE DRUG

Continued use of cocaine can cause serious physical damage to the user's body. For example, myocardial infarction (which occurs when the heart is damaged by a lack of blood flow to the heart muscle), sudden death from respiratory or cardiac arrest, and stroke have been associated with cocaine use among young and otherwise healthy persons. These probably occur because cocaine raises blood pressure, narrows blood vessels, and alters the electrical activity of the heart. A cocaine user's heart has to work harder and faster to pump blood through the body. This physical stress may trigger chest pains or a heart attack—even in someone with an apparently healthy heart. Although there is a persistent myth that nobody gets addicted or killed by trying cocaine just once, the truth is that even a first-time user takes the risk of dying of a heart attack, stroke, or respiratory failure.

Lung infections, as noted above, are frequently seen in users who smoke cocaine or crack, since the damaged tissue of their lungs is more vulnerable than a healthy person's. Cocaine or crack smokers are likely to develop diseases such as emphysema or tuberculosis. Symptoms of these diseases include coughing up thick mucus and blood, wheezing, and difficulty breathing. Infections can also result from performing special breathing maneuvers to better absorb cocaine that has been inhaled. The impure cocaine powder being inhaled into already-damaged lungs exposes the tissue to all kinds of toxins and irritants. Chest pain is a common symptom, caused by the damage to either heart or lung tissue as both organs undergo more stress to keep the body functioning.

Using cocaine can damage the brain by disturbing the brain's electrical signals, causing seizures. Sometimes these seizures affect the most basic systems of the brain—the ones that control heartbeat and breathing—and lead to cardiac arrest or respiratory failure. In addition, the increase in blood pressure caused by narrowed veins and increased heart rate may trigger a stroke, rupturing blood vessels in the brain and causing the victim to lose some brain function permanently, if

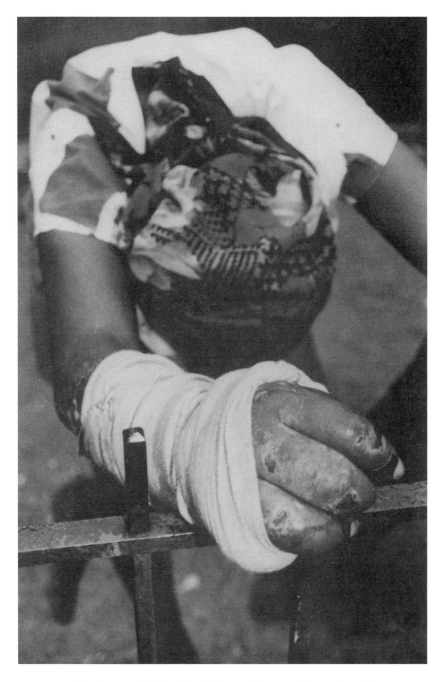

A woman waits to be searched by police during a raid on a crack house in Washington, D.C. The infection and swelling on her hand and arm is a result of her habit of injecting drugs.

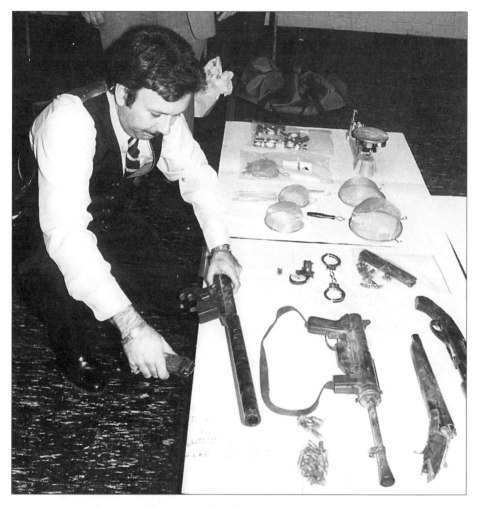

A detective examines some of the weapons found in the apartment of two men suspected of running a "cocaine factory." The two men had been killed, apparently by other drug dealers. Violence is common when drugs such as cocaine are involved.

it doesn't kill the person. Often, stroke victims who survive suffer partial paralysis.

Users who inject cocaine or who also abuse alcohol—studies have shown that a large percentage of cocaine users also use other drugs—risk liver damage. One of the liver's functions is to remove toxins from the blood, and the repeated stress of attempting to clean cocaine out of the bloodstream can cause the liver to deteriorate.

COCAINE AND VIOLENCE

The "markets" where cocaine is bought and sold tend to be violent, dangerous places. There is no legal recourse for someone who believes that he or she has been "ripped off" in an exchange for cocaine, so dealers resort to violence to settle scores and to keep control of their markets. This practice, although seen to some degree with all illegal drugs, is especially severe in the case of cocaine and crack because of the degree of organization of the cocaine "business" and the large amounts of money involved. Drug-related stabbings and shootings are common, whether to intimidate potential rivals in the dealing business or to punish someone who may have attempted to steal drugs or drug money from the dealer. These attacks can prove especially damaging to users: because of the increase in heart rate and blood pressure, cocaine users who suffer traumatic injuries are likely to bleed more and be at greater risk of going into shock than if they were healthy.

INCREASED RISK OF AIDS

Human Immunodeficiency Virus (HIV), the virus that causes AIDS, is one of the most serious possible consequences of using cocaine. HIV is transmitted through sexual contact with an infected person, or contact with an infected person's blood (including the traces of blood on a used hypodermic needle or in a syringe). The virus frequently cannot be detected by blood tests for six to nine months after infection occurs, and symptoms may not appear for months or even years afterward. Thus, seemingly healthy people may, in fact, be infected with the virus but not yet have full-blown AIDS. They may not even be aware that they carry the virus and may not take the precautions necessary to avoid spreading the disease to anyone else, continuing to have unsafe sex or to share needles.

The highest rate of HIV infection among cocaine users is among those who inject the drug intravenously. Many intravenous drug users share needles with other addicts; if one of the users of a needle is infected with HIV or another blood-transmitted disease (such as hepatitis), anyone else who uses that needle is actually injecting the disease along with the drug. While there are sterilization procedures to rid needles and syringes of possible contamination, many users do not know how to perform them or do not bother. Use of infected needles only affects users who inject cocaine, but any cocaine addict may

Darryl Strawberry, once considered a possible Hall-of-Fame baseball player, struggled to come back in the sport after a long suspension for failing drug tests.

engage in promiscuous and unsafe sexual behavior, which increases the risk of AIDS and other sexually transmitted diseases, such as syphilis and gonorrhea. Users may not know or care who they are having sex with while they are on cocaine, and use of the drug tends to make people less likely to take safe-sex precautions with any partner. Some users also turn to prostitution in order to get money to buy the drug, increasing their likelihood of exposure even more.

COCAINE AND ATHLETES

One of the ironies of cocaine use is that it is seen so often among professional sports stars—people who are often paid multimillion dollar salaries to be in top physical and mental shape. In addition to Len Bias, there are a number of other examples of professional athletes whose reputations and careers have been damaged by their use of the drug.

In 1995 Roy Tarpley, the center for the Dallas Mavericks basketball team, was thrown out of the NBA for using cocaine and violating the antidrug policy. Tarpley had already been suspended once for using cocaine, and the second offense voided his contract, which would have paid him $23 million over the next five years. "Roy was given every opportunity to succeed," said Norm Sonju, Mavericks president and general manager. "This is the final chapter. The book is finished."

Star outfielder Darryl Strawberry was also suspended from professional baseball in the early 1990s for failing drug tests. He was ordered to pay $350,000 in fines and placed under house arrest. When he was permitted to return to professional baseball, it was for a salary about one-fourth of what he'd made prior to his suspension. In September 1995 Sammie Smith, a one-time Florida State running back and a first-round draft pick of the Miami Dolphins in 1989, was arrested and charged with being a major supplier of crack cocaine. A videotape played in court showed Smith discussing the drug business with an undercover agent. As the judge denied bail, he remarked to Smith's defense attorneys, "You say he is a person with a good reputation. But it's a reputation he enjoyed prior to his arrest, and for other reasons."

Cocaine use in the sports world is not limited to the United States, either. In August 1996 English cricket player Ed Giddins was suspended from the game for two years after being found guilty of taking cocaine. The committee reviewing the case noted that use of an illegal drug was "a grave breach of regulations which was not only likely to bring the game into disrepute but which had the potential to put at risk the safety of fellow players and officials." The report concluded that "cricket, its players and administrators, would not tolerate in its ranks those who indulge in the use of a prohibited drug. The committee was sure the public would demand nothing less." That same year, Argentine soccer idol Diego Maradona, the hero of Argentina's 1986 World Cup championship team, gave evidence during his manager's trial for cocaine dealing and drug possession. Maradona had previously admitted his own cocaine habit.

From these few examples, it's easy to see how dangerous crack and cocaine can be. Even a professional athlete, whose lifestyle and career depend on a healthy mind working within a healthy body, can fall victim to the seductive and addictive qualities of cocaine and crack.

COCAINE AND PREGNANCY

One of the most horrifying aspects of cocaine use is its effects on those who cannot control it: the infants born to mothers addicted to cocaine. Cocaine use by pregnant women can lead to serious physical and mental problems in their children.

Virtually any substance that a pregnant woman takes into her body is passed on to the developing fetus through the placenta. In a healthy mother, this allows the nutrients in her food to nourish her child. In a cocaine-addicted mother, however, this allows the drug to be passed on just as easily. The drug inhibits the natural development of the fetus by decreasing the flow of blood to the baby, thus decreasing the amount of nutrients and oxygen that the child receives. It is believed that that decrease in blood flow has caused numerous birth defects and abnormalities, as well as miscarriages and stillbirths. Also, because a cocaine addict is usually more concerned with obtaining the drug than food, a poor cocaine addict's baby may be further malnourished by a simple lack of nutrients in his or her mother's blood. If a woman injects cocaine, or any other drug, her baby faces the same risk of contracting HIV as she does.

Birth may be a more difficult and dangerous process for a cocaine-addicted mother than for a healthy woman; the drug often causes increased bleeding and risk of shock for the mother when the placenta is separated from the womb. Cocaine-affected babies are frequently born premature and with extremely low birth weights (less than two pounds in some cases), and sometimes with organs unformed or deformed. Many cocaine-exposed babies are difficult to nurse or take care of and run a high risk of seizures or sudden infant death syndrome. Hospital care for infants born addicted to cocaine or born with cocaine-related problems can cost thousands of dollars per day, an amount that most addicts do not have and are not willing to spend, causing many of the babies to be abandoned at the hospital.

The widespread use of crack cocaine among poor residents of inner cities has led to the birth of thousands of "crack babies" whose prenatal exposure to the drug leaves them with severe emotional and neurological problems. Many of these children are now school-age, and studies have shown them to have emotional difficulties, behavioral disorders, and moderate to severe learning disabilities, suggesting that they suffered permanent neurological damage as a result of drug use by their mother. In some large cities, such as Los Angeles, New York, and Philadelphia, enrollment in special-education classes has increased, and sometimes even doubled, as a result of these children's special learning needs.

Cocaine and crack use can radically change the way the user thinks, acts, and sees the world. For many users, coming down is marked by feelings of apathy, depression, or edginess.

5

COCAINE AND CRACK: THE PSYCHOLOGICAL EFFECTS

The American Psychiatric Association classifies two groups of disorders caused by the use of drugs. The two groups are substance-use disorders (that is, disorders involving patterns of using the substance), and substance-induced disorders (that is, disorders involving the way the substance changes the user's mental functioning). While there are only two defined cocaine-use disorders (cocaine abuse and cocaine dependence), there are many cocaine-induced disorders, including cocaine intoxication, cocaine withdrawal, cocaine-induced psychotic disorder with delusions or hallucinations, cocaine intoxication delirium, cocaine-induced mood disorder, cocaine-induced anxiety disorder, cocaine-induced sexual dysfunction, and cocaine-induced sleep disorder.

COCAINE-USE DISORDERS

Crack and cocaine use change the way a person acts and thinks. And because cocaine has extremely powerful, and exhilarating, effects, individuals that use the drug can develop dependence after a very short period of time. Research has shown that in many cases, the pattern of dependence begins to form with the first use.

This is even true in animals. In studies that used animals to determine the physical, psychological, and social harm that cocaine causes, every species that was tested (rats, dogs, and monkeys) learned to take the cocaine for no reward other than the effects of the drug. The animals preferred higher to lower doses, ate almost nothing, and suffered serious health effects when they had unlimited access to the cocaine.

Cocaine abuse is less severe than cocaine dependence. Use, neglect of responsibilities, and interpersonal conflict often occur around paydays or special occasions, resulting in brief periods (hours to a few days) of high-dose use, followed by much longer periods (weeks to months) of occasional use or abstinence. Because of the highly addictive qualities of cocaine, abuse usually progresses fairly rapidly to dependence (as seen with the animals in the lab study above). When the problems associated with abuse occur along with signs of tolerance, withdrawal when use is suspended, or compulsive behavior related to obtaining and using cocaine, the diagnosis of cocaine dependence instead of abuse is applied.

Smoking cocaine or crack or injecting the drug tend to be particularly associated with a rapid progression from use to abuse or dependence, often occurring over a period of only a few short weeks. Snorting can lead to a more gradual progression, usually occurring over months to years. Regardless of the way the drug is used, tolerance, and eventually dependence, occurs with repeated use.

Cocaine dependence is generally seen in either of two patterns of self-administration: episodic (occasional) and daily or almost daily use. In the episodic pattern, the cocaine use tends to be separated by two or more days of nonuse. For example, there may be intense use over a weekend or on one or more weekdays.

A "binge" is an extreme form of episodic use that typically involves continuous high-dose use over a period of hours or days. These binges are often associated with dependence. The binges usually end only when cocaine supplies are all consumed and are then followed by an intense "crash," or period of withdrawal.

Chronic daily use may involve either high or low doses. Chronic use may take place throughout the day or be restricted to only a few hours. In chronic daily use, there are generally no wide fluctuations in dose on successive days, but there is often a gradual increase in dose over time.

An early sign of cocaine dependence is when the user finds it increasingly difficult to resist using cocaine whenever it is available. Dependence can be so strong that the user may experience cravings on seeing any white powderlike substance, from corn starch and flour to talcum powder. Since white powders are fairly common in everyday life, this can make withdrawal and treatment extremely difficult. And because of cocaine's brief intoxication period, there is a need for frequent dosing to maintain a high.

Cocaine-use disorders are often associated with dependence on or abuse of other substances, especially alcohol, marijuana, and depressants, which are often taken to reduce the anxiety and other unpleasant stimulant side effects of cocaine. The danger here is that the body receives mixed messages from stimulant and depressant agents at the same time.

One of the factors that makes cocaine so dangerous is the rapid progression from abuse to dependence. Users soon feel that they need the drug, often at the expense of all other interests in their lives.

Cocaine dependence may also be associated with a number of other disorders:

- post-traumatic stress disorder, in which a person develops anxiety, depression, or changed behavior patterns after a particularly traumatic event, in an attempt to avoid facing the event and its consequences.

- antisocial personality disorder, in which the individual displays a pattern of consistent disregard for others, including violence and/or violations of others' rights

- attention-deficit/hyperactivity disorder, in which the person is unable to concentrate or becomes hyperactive, or unable to get settled physically or psychologically.

These disorders will be defined more fully at the end of this chapter.

Although cocaine and crack are relatively inexpensive, persons with cocaine dependence can easily spend extremely large amounts of money on the drug within a very short period of time in an attempt to maintain the high. As a result, the person using the substance may request frequent salary advances if employed or may become involved in illegal activities like theft, prostitution, or drug dealing to obtain funds to purchase the drug. Important responsibilities such as work, study, or child care may be grossly neglected to obtain or use cocaine.

Dependence is commonly associated with a gradual tolerance to the desirable effects of cocaine, which leads to taking larger doses. However, with continuing use, there is a steady lessening of pleasurable effects and a steady increase in negative emotional reactions caused by tolerance.

COCAINE INTOXICATION AND WITHDRAWAL

Cocaine intoxication usually begins with a high feeling, which can include a whole range of symptoms, such as euphoria with enhanced vigor; markedly increased outgoing behavior or talkativeness; hyperactivity; restlessness; excessive watchfulness; interpersonal sensitivity; anxiety; tension; alertness; pompous or pretentious behavior; stereotyped and repetitive behavior; anger; and impaired judgment. Any combination of these symptoms may be seen.

The extent of the changes in the way a user may act and think depend on many different factors. These include the amount of the dose used and the individual characteristics of the person taking it (for example, if the person is a chronic user, if the person has mixed the cocaine with other drugs, and so on).

Stimulant effects such as euphoria, increased pulse and blood pressure, and increased psychomotor activity (that is, movement or muscular activity associated with mental processes) are most commonly seen. Acute intoxication with high doses of cocaine may be associated with rambling speech, headache, and tinnitus (ringing in the ears). There may also be paranoia (the feeling that everyone is "out to get you"), auditory hallucinations ("hearing things"), and tactile, or felt, hallucinations. The user may or may not realize that these symptoms are caused by using the drug. Depressant effects such as sadness, fatigue, slowed heart rate, lowered blood pressure, and decreased psychomotor activity are less common and generally emerge only with ongoing high-dose use. Whether acute or chronic, cocaine intoxication is often associated with impaired social or occupational functioning. Intoxication is usually accompanied by two or more of the physical signs and symptoms noted in the previous chapter.

Diagnosing cocaine intoxication in a patient is based on four relatively basic guidelines. These include recent use of cocaine by the patient, behavioral or psychological changes as noted above, two or more of the physical symptoms noted previously, and the absence of another medical or mental condition that could cause the same symptoms. Recent use of cocaine is the key factor.

Withdrawal is a cocaine-induced disorder caused by the cessation of, or abrupt reduction in, cocaine use that has been heavy and prolonged enough to lead to dependence. Typically, the symptoms of withdrawal include a feeling of depression or apathy; vivid, unpleasant dreams; insomnia (the inability to sleep) or hypersomnia (sleeping all the time); increased appetite; and psychomotor agitation or retardation. Acute cases of withdrawal can also include severe muscle cramps and nausea. Most users will experience drug cravings while in withdrawal, and many also feel an inability to take pleasure in anything around them. After a cocaine binge, a user will typically experience acute withdrawal, which can last for several days and cause such a depressed mood that the user may consider or attempt suicide. Cocaine withdrawal is very difficult to predict in intensity or duration, however, and a few users never experience withdrawal symptoms at all.

OTHER COCAINE-INDUCED DISORDERS

Cocaine intoxication and cocaine withdrawal are distinguished from other cocaine-induced disorders because the symptoms of the other disorders are far more excessive or severe than is usually seen in cocaine intoxication and withdrawal. In the other cocaine-induced disorders, the symptoms are severe enough to warrant independent clinical attention—that is, to be treated for themselves as well as being considered a result of cocaine use.

Hallucinations are very common in cocaine users. They may believe they hear, see, or even feel things that aren't there. A common tactile hallucination occurs when the cocaine user feels thousands of imaginary insects ("coke bugs") running up and down the arms either on or beneath the skin. The user scratches wildly at his or her arms to brush off these invisible "bugs," often cutting and damaging the skin on the arms.

Individuals with cocaine dependence often have temporary depressive symptoms, panic attacks (sudden overwhelming feelings of fear or panic), social-phobic type behavior (being afraid to be around other people), and general anxiety. Eating disorders or anorexia-like symptoms are also common, with weight loss and lack of appetite often seen because of cocaine's ability to suppress the appetite at the same time that it speeds up a person's metabolism.

Both crack and cocaine use can cause "cocaine psychosis"—violent, erratic, or paranoid behavior—although it appears more rapidly in crack users. Sufferers may become anxious, believe they have superhuman powers, or become suspicious or paranoid to the point that they believe their lives are in danger. A user with cocaine psychosis may behave violently for no apparent reason, or attempt impossible feats, such as jumping off a rooftop or out of a window in the mistaken belief that he or she can fly. Erratic behavior, social isolation, and sexual dysfunction—the inability to perform sexually—are often seen in long-term cocaine dependence.

One of the most extreme instances of cocaine toxicity is cocaine-induced psychotic disorder, which can involve delusions and hallucinations that resemble a paranoid-type schizophrenia (see below). Users may persist in ridiculous false beliefs, such as thinking a conspiracy of people are "watching" or "out to get them," or they may see, hear, or feel disturbing hallucinations, which can cause them to become violent. Mental disturbances that occur in association with cocaine use usually resolve within hours to days after cessation of use, although they can persist for weeks.

COCAINE AND OTHER MENTAL DISORDERS

Cocaine-induced disorders may be characterized by symptoms that indicate a primary mental disorder. For example, the depression caused by cocaine use may be similar to another depressive condition. The marked mental disturbances that can result from the effects of cocaine may also be similar to the symptoms of paranoid-type schizophrenia; bipolar and other mood disorders; post-traumatic stress disorder; antisocial personality disorder; attention deficit/hyperactivity disorder; and generalized anxiety and panic disorders.

Schizophrenia is a psychotic disorder usually characterized by

Often, cocaine users experience feelings of paranoia or heightened sensitivity; they may falsely believe that people are "out to get them" or that others are mocking them.

Use of cocaine can cause problems among family members to become more intense or unpleasant. Ironically, some people start taking the drug as a way to "escape" from the very problems it worsens.

withdrawal from reality; illogical patterns of thinking; "flattening" or lack of emotions; chaotic or disorganized speech; delusions; halluci- nations, including "hearing voices"; and accompanied in varying degrees by other behavioral or intellectual disturbances. The word "schizophrenia" means "splitting of the mind," suggesting the frac- tured way schizophrenics relate to the world around them. A popular misconception is that schizophrenia involves a "split personality," but that is actually a different and far more rare condition. The most dis- tinctive feature of schizophrenia, psychiatrists now believe, is patients' complete inability to relate to or understand life in a normal, sane way. Cocaine use can cause symptoms similar to the paranoid type of schizophrenia, in which a person suffers from delusions of grandeur or persecution (often persecution by a large organization such as the

FBI, or even by an alien race). These delusions may be extremely elaborate and clearly defined, and the person may even claim to have proof that they are true.

Bipolar mood disorder, also known as manic-depressive disorder, is a severe mental disorder involving manic episodes (characterized by an abnormally elevated or irritable mood, grandiosity, sleeplessness, extravagance, and a tendency toward irrational judgment) that frequently alternate with episodes of depression (possibly including lethargy, a sense of worthlessness, lack of concentration, suicidal thoughts, disrupted sleeping patterns, and guilt). There are several different subtypes of bipolar disorder, involving different combinations of manic and depressive symptoms. Bipolar disorder can be extremely dangerous if untreated; an estimated 15 percent of people with the disorder attempt suicide at some point in their lives.

Post-traumatic stress disorder involves a series of symptoms caused by the shock of witnessing or experiencing a traumatic or horrible event, such as being injured in battle or witnessing the violent death of a loved one. Typically, people with post-traumatic stress disorder suffer from persistent and vivid recollections of the trauma and feel immense distress when exposed to anything that might symbolize or resemble aspects of the original traumatic event. The person will try to avoid any stimuli that might bring on these recollections and will sometimes develop a limited amnesia surrounding the event. Many times these people find it difficult to have relationships with others or to enjoy activities that previously held their interest, and they often show symptoms of anxiety.

Antisocial personality disorder, characterized by a persistent pattern of disregard for others or violations of their rights, begins in childhood or adolescence and continues on into adulthood. People with this disorder may express contempt for others around them, lack empathy or any feeling for others, and have an inflated sense of their own worth or position, often expressed as superficial, condescending charm. They frequently have difficulty coping with boredom and controlling their impulses and may complain of tension or mood swings. Violence and abuse of people close to them are other common behaviors.

Attention deficit/hyperactivity disorder (ADHD) typically begins in childhood and is marked by problems with inattention, hyperactivity, and/or impulsivity. People with this disorder may be unable to keep themselves from being distracted, unable to sit still, or unable to wait

Depression is often felt at the end of a cocaine high or "binge." After long-term drug use, depression may become a chronic state that the addict has difficulty escaping.

for anything. Frequently ADHD causes difficulty interacting in environments such as school or work, where some degree of order must be maintained. ADHD is believed to be caused by genetic or neurological factors and can sometimes be controlled with medication. In many cases, children of women who used cocaine during pregnancy develop ADHD or similar problems in childhood.

Generalized anxiety and panic disorders are characterized simply by overwhelming fear and tension, and persistent worry or feelings of terror. They may be brought on by specific situations (taking a test or going somewhere unfamiliar, for example), or they may happen at random times, without any noticeable trigger. The most common symptom of these disorders is a "panic attack," during which the person may experience increased heart rate, sweating, chest pain, or difficulty breathing. The intensity and duration of the negative emotion or reaction is disproportionate to the seriousness of any triggering situation or event.

Cocaine use can obviously affect the mind in many ways. It is important to understand that no matter how good that first high may have felt, long-term use can cause a complete break with reality.

A father visits his son at a residential drug treatment center designed to help teens break their patterns of substance dependence and put their lives back together.

6

TREATMENT AND THERAPY

Probably every person who starts to take drugs thinks that he or she can quit at any time. Often, users do not realize how addictive crack or cocaine can be until they are unable to quit using them by themselves. Fortunately there are several options available for people who need help to stop using cocaine, ranging from 12-step programs like Narcotics Anonymous (NA) to clinical therapy with medication. There are both residential (or live-in) and outpatient treatments, and different therapies can help people with all levels of addiction, treating the withdrawal symptoms and psychological problems they may face when quitting.

WITHDRAWAL

The first step a user experiences when he or she tries to quit is withdrawal, which occurs within a few hours after ending or reducing cocaine use that has been heavy and prolonged. Cocaine withdrawal syndrome is distinguished by extreme depression plus any combination of the following symptoms: fatigue, vivid and unpleasant dreams, insomnia or hypersomnia, increased appetite, and changes in the level of psychomotor activity. A decreased sense of pleasure and intense drug craving can often be present as well, but they are not part of the diagnostic criteria. As we noted previously, individuals with cocaine dependence often develop conditioned responses to cocaine-related stimuli, such as the craving for cocaine on seeing any white powderlike substance. These responses will usually be the most intense during a period of withdrawal, as the user's brain and body try to adjust to the absence of cocaine, but they can recur at intervals for long periods of time and often contribute to a relapse.

Acute withdrawal symptoms (a crash) are often seen after periods of repetitive high-dose use ("runs" or binges). These periods are characterized by intense and unpleasant feelings of fatigue and depression and generally require several days of rest and recuperation. Clinical depressive symptoms with suicidal thoughts or behavior can also occur. These suicidal thoughts are generally the most serious problem seen during crashing or other forms of cocaine withdrawal.

It is important in diagnosing cocaine withdrawal to be sure that these symptoms are not caused by a general medical condition and are not better accounted for by another mental disorder. Therefore, the following criteria are used to help a health care professional diagnose cocaine withdrawal:

- ending or reducing cocaine use that has been heavy and prolonged
- negative, depressed mood and two (or more) of the following physiological changes, developing within a few hours to several days after reduced use: fatigue; vivid, unpleasant dreams; insomnia or hypersomnia; increased appetite; psychomotor retardation or agitation
- the symptoms above causing clinically significant distress or impairment in social, occupational, or other important areas of functioning
- an indication that these symptoms are not caused by a general medical condition and are not better accounted for by another mental disorder.

METHODS OF TREATMENT

Treatment begins with the process of detoxification, ridding the body of the drug. During the detoxification process, the user will experience withdrawal symptoms as the body adjusts to the sudden absence of the substance to which it has grown accustomed. In some cases medications such as antidepressants are used to help treat the severe depression that occurs during withdrawal, as well as the underlying psychological problems that can lead a person to attempt to "self-medicate" with cocaine.

There are several different methods of treatment to help the user successfully detoxify and stay clean. For less severely addicted users, an outpatient program of therapy may be effective. The recovering addict can schedule two or three sessions per week with a therapist, or meetings

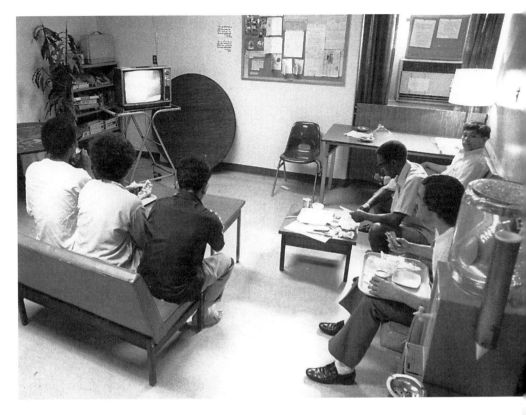

For severely addicted persons, a program of live-in treatment is often the only way to turn their lives around. In the treatment center, most of their activities are structured around becoming and remaining drug-free.

with a support group, to help reinforce the resolve to quit; the rest of the user's time is spent at home or at work or in other everyday pursuits. Most treatment programs are outpatient-oriented. For more long-term or severely addicted users, a residential program of treatment normally has a more lasting effect, allowing the user to detoxify and rehabilitate in a controlled, drug-free environment without any of the stimuli that the addict associates with using cocaine. In a residential treatment program, the recovering addict lives in the treatment facility, which might be a hospital, group home, or halfway house. Most of the residents' time is spent in treatment-related activities, including therapy sessions, job and parenting-skills training, and contributing to the maintenance of the facility.

MARION BARRY:
RECOVERING ADDICT

In the 1960s, a civil rights activist from Memphis, Tennessee, named Marion Barry came to Washington, D.C., to champion the fight against segregation and discrimination. He first entered city politics as a leader of the Student Non-violent Coordinating Committee, for which he organized protests. In the 1970s, Barry won his first elected positions, becoming first a school board member and then an at-large councilman when the city gained home rule in 1974. In 1978 he was elected to his first term as mayor.

Barry would serve as mayor of the District of Columbia for three consecutive terms, leading the city through difficult economic times and a bid for statehood in the early 1980s and pioneering a new jobs program for city youth. During his second and third terms, however, personal scandals began to surface, first simply as rumors that he was using drugs, then allegations that he was involved in extramarital affairs. Finally, in a Federal Bureau of Investigation sting at the Vista Hotel, Barry was videotaped smoking crack cocaine in the company of a former girlfriend in January of 1990.

At the trial, prosecutors sought conviction on 14 separate charges of drug possession and use, both on the night of the sting operation and on several previous occasions. The jury, feeling that some of the charges were unfair and that the sting may have been an attempt at entrapment, only found Barry guilty of a single misdemeanor possession charge. Barry was sentenced to six months in prison and required to pay a fine of $5,000. His wife, Effi, separated from him as a result of the scandal and allegations of his infidelity.

The conviction and the separation seemed to signal to Barry that he needed to turn his life around. In 1992, after serving his sentence and completing a rehabilitation course, he successfully campaigned for a city council seat, and in 1994 he remarried, to a political science professor named Cora Masters. Later that year he was reelected to an unprecedented fourth term as mayor. Barry credits his faith and the help and support of his family and friends with enabling him to overcome his drug problems and find the strength to face the challenges of his office.

Washington, D.C., mayor Marion Barry arrives at U.S. District Court at the beginning of his trial for cocaine possession. Barry was convicted on one misdemeanor count of possession of cocaine. After he had served his jail time and completed a recovery program, he successfully campaigned for reelection.

Because cocaine causes such potent feelings of false well-being and self-confidence, many users come to be dependent on it to instill those feelings. Without the drug, they may feel as if they are not as likable or not as capable as they were when they were high. Most treatment programs address this effect as one of their primary targets, trying to help users find a sense of self-esteem that depends on their own accomplishments and skills rather than the presence of cocaine. Vocational training or educational programs may help this process, giving the user new skills and knowledge to lean on and to form a healthy alternative to the inflated feelings cocaine can cause. Many residential therapy programs try to help recovering addicts find new interests in their communities that do not involve drug use. Group therapy sessions or self-help meetings such as NA or Cocaine Anonymous can also help to build this self-esteem, showing recovering addicts that others care what happens to them and that they don't need drugs to make them feel important. Just as peers and family may influence the likelihood for taking drugs, supportive family members and friends can help lead the way to a successful recovery.

Patients who enter residential treatment programs, especially, will need the help of their families and friends when the residential treatment is over. To avoid the stimuli that can trigger a conditioned response, recovering addicts must learn new ways of socializing once they leave the treatment center. They must try to avoid social involvement with current cocaine users, as the pressure of their drug habits may influence someone in recovery. This lifestyle change can be very difficult for someone who lives in an environment where cocaine use is prevalent; if there is any way for a recovering addict to get out of a house or neighborhood where cocaine is used or sold regularly, he or she should do so.

There is no single standard treatment for cocaine addiction. Different programs use different combinations of psychotherapy, medication, behavioral therapy, and peer group support. Because patients in treatment can have addictions of such varied severity, it is unlikely that there will ever be a single treatment program that works for all addicts. However, as research continues, therapists are learning more about what combinations are most effective for each level of addiction. For example, researchers have found that participation in a support group such as NA makes a user more likely to remain drug-free after other therapy has ended. In one study, patients who otherwise came from

A support group ends its meeting with a pledge to help each other stay clean. In an out-patient treatment like this one, a good support network is essential to recovery.

similar conditions were more likely to be drug-free six months after therapy if they had been attending NA meetings for at least three months after therapy.

Regardless of the treatment program, many users believe they can return to occasional use of cocaine. However, they frequently find that "occasional use" becomes a return to their former addictive patterns of behavior. Much like an alcoholic who is in remission or recovering, a cocaine addict must learn to accept the fact that not using the drug for several months or years is not necessarily a sign that he or she is "cured," and that it is never safe for him or her to use cocaine "just one more time." Former cocaine users must continue to lead a drug-free lifestyle to gain and maintain control of their lives.

This month, 8 million Americans will go jogging, 7 million will play tennis, and 6 million will do cocaine.

A few of those 6 million may be your patients.

You may have trouble recognizing cocaine abuse because there are few visible symptoms. Often the only way to find out is to ask the right questions.

Any cocaine use is potential *abuse*. Give your patients who have a problem the 1-800-COCAINE hotline or the National Institute on Drug Abuse information and referral line (1-800-662-HELP).

PARTNERSHIP FOR A DRUG-FREE AMERICA

deltakos USA

Healthcare Division
of J. Walter Thompson

A poster from a public awareness campaign highlights the extent of the cocaine problem in the United States. Millions of other people who interact with cocaine users will also be affected by their drug habits.

7

COCAINE'S IMPACT ON SOCIETY

Cocaine's effects can be devastating not only to the user, but also to anyone else in the user's environment. The drug can cause poor work performance, contribute to violence and crime, destroy the user's relationships with other people, and ruin school performance. Many users lose their jobs, alienate their loved ones, and end up in prison because of their cocaine habits. In this way, the use of cocaine by a few people can have unpleasant consequences for many others in their society as a whole.

COCAINE ON THE JOB

Individuals with cocaine dependence have been known to spend thousands of dollars on the substance within very short periods of time. This spending causes financial catastrophes in which jobs, savings, or homes have been lost. A user may be working only to afford the drug that makes him or her a bad employee.

A recent study found that workers who use cocaine were:

- 1.5 times as likely as nonusers to have had an accident
- nearly twice as likely to have been injured
- more than twice as likely to have been absent.

With all the concerns about drug-related incidents in the workplace, many employers will not hire drug users and will fire employees found to be using drugs. Some workplaces have random drug-testing policies to try to ensure that they keep drug users out of their workforces. Thousands of young people have been refused entry into military service because they have drug use histories or did not pass a urine screening for drug use.

Participants in a conference sponsored by NIDA on drugs in the workplace identified three major areas of concern about drug use and work. These are: concern about safety in high-precision or high-risk occupations (such as air traffic controllers, truck or bus drivers, flight crews, construction workers, and medical care workers); concerns about productivity, including poorly manufactured products and understaffed businesses or services (this may also include morale problems seen in workers who must pick up the slack for an absent coworker); and concern about the overall health of the workforce, including increases in health care and insurance costs.

Some employers, realizing how easy it is to be lured into a drug habit and how hard it is to quit, have begun sponsoring rehabilitation programs for their workers. An employee might receive a suspension from work and an order to go through treatment instead of simply being fired. While this option might not convince every cocaine user to quit, many have found it an incentive to stop using the drug before it ruins their lives.

COCAINE, CRIME, AND VIOLENCE

Cocaine is an illegal drug, and individuals may engage in criminal activities to obtain money to buy it. Also, drug users are often victimized because use of the drug impairs judgment and the ability to take care of oneself in dangerous situations.

People who buy and sell drugs are attractive targets for violence because they are thought to have large amounts of money or drugs with them. And, because drug dealing and use is illegal, violence in the drug-dealing or -using community is less likely to be reported to the police.

Violence is also associated with the cocaine "trade," both in the United States and abroad. The violence associated with the drug trade in South America (especially the drug cartels described in Chapter 1) is well known. However, as shipment and smuggling activities have become more sophisticated, the violence has spread. Dealers of cocaine may use violence as a means of deterring rivals from attempting to sell drugs in the same area or as a way of punishing others in their supply networks who have broken an agreement on money or drugs. This violence is particularly severe in the case of cocaine (as opposed to other illegal drugs, such as marijuana) because the markets are so unstable and because the stakes—both in money to be made and in penalties suffered by those who are arrested—are so high.

Cocaine use can also cause a person to exhibit irrational, aggressive behavior. Extreme anger with threats or acting out of aggressive

Police round up suspected drug users in a sweep of one of New York City's most drug-infested areas. High levels of drug use in a neighborhood generally cause violent crime rates to rise, decreasing the quality of life for everyone in the area.

behavior may occur; often, a person who is high on cocaine will have a false sense of invulnerability, which can fuel the desire to pick a fight or use violent, aggressive means to get what he or she wants. Mood changes such as depression, suicidal thoughts, irritability, inability to feel pleasure, emotional instability, or disturbances in attention and concentration are common, especially during cocaine withdrawal.

INCREASED DRUG-RELATED VIOLENCE IN THE CARIBBEAN

Since 1994 the Caribbean islands have seen increased drug trade, with many islands used as cocaine shipment bases by South American drug lords. The U. S. Drug Enforcement Agency (DEA) believes that many traffickers use the islands as storage and distribution points for both the U.S. and European markets.

According to a 1996 *Time* magazine article, a series of drug-related disappearances and murders on the island of St. Kitts is directly linked to the cocaine trade. A former ambassador to the United Nations from St. Kitts, who was implicated in a scheme to launder drug money, vanished while on a fishing trip with his wife and four friends. In another case, the son of a deputy prime minister suspected of stealing from smugglers was slain with his girlfriend; while investigating the case, the island's police superintendent was assassinated.

Informants or witnesses who testify against the leaders of drug cartels on the island of Trinidad "have a way of getting killed, their jaws shot off, their food poisoned, or their families executed," the 1996 *Time* article said. In 1993, police officers from Scotland Yard who were investigating police corruption in Trinidad had to seek refuge in a Hilton Hotel after gunmen threatened them—inside police headquarters.

Increased drug use and violence are also being seen in Puerto Rico, which, as a U.S. commonwealth, has light customs checks for people and cargo entering the United States. Once cocaine or other drugs are smuggled into Puerto Rico, they can easily be transported to cities in the mainland United States. "San Juan has become what Miami used to be," American attorney Guillermo Gil, who was the victim of a carjacking by a teenager high on crack, told *Time*. "People are afraid to go out at night."

As noted in previous chapters, cocaine users may also suffer greater physical damage and risk from violent injuries. A cocaine user who suffers a traumatic injury such as a shooting or stabbing is likely to bleed more, and is more likely to go into a state of shock than a nonuser. These factors combined with the prevalence of violence in the cocaine trade make use of the drug even more risky.

Drug users and drug dealers make up a high percentage of the inmates in U.S. prisons. In 1995, the Bureau of Justice Statistics reported that 61 percent of inmates in federal prisons and 21 percent of inmates in state prisons had been convicted of a drug-related offense.

COCAINE AND THE LAW

Federal law classifies cocaine as a narcotic, even though it is technically a stimulant (opiates and other depressive drugs are narcotics). This classification stems from the Harrison Narcotics Act of 1914, which was intended to restrict the manufacture and use of drugs commonly abused at the time, including both opiates and cocaine. Even today, the word narcotic (meaning "inducing sleep or numbness") is often used to refer to any illegal drug.

The Controlled Substances Act, passed in 1970, provides the basis for modern federal laws to regulate psychoactive drugs. Under the act, two federal agencies—the Food and Drug Administration and the Drug Enforcement Administration—classify drugs into five different categories, or schedules. Drugs in Schedule I are considered the most harmful or likely to be abused, with no medical use; drugs in Schedule V are the least likely to be abused and can be purchased over the counter. Cocaine is classified as a Schedule II drug, which means that it is considered to have a "high potential for abuse," with high likelihood of abuse leading to physical or psychological dependence, but there is also some acceptable medical use. (In the case of cocaine, the medical use is as a local anesthetic for some surgical procedures.)

Federal sentencing guidelines for possession of less than 50 grams of powder cocaine include a jail term of up to one year, a fine of $1,000 to $5,000, or both. Repeat offenses or larger quantities of cocaine lead to longer jail terms or higher fines. The penalties for crack cocaine are harsher: a first-time offender prosecuted for crack possession under federal law faces a mandatory minimum sentence of 5 years in prison, and up to 20 years is possible, in addition to fines.

The disparity between sentences for powder and crack cocaine offenders has caused some controversy. Some people argue that the differing guidelines are racially biased, because the majority of people prosecuted for powder possession are white, whereas the majority of people prosecuted for crack possession are black, and they face longer sentences for the same amount of the drug. Opponents of the sentencing laws point out that powder cocaine is the essential ingredient in crack cocaine and that what causes the severe punishment is not the possession of cocaine, but the choice of the drug's form: the method more common among blacks is being punished many times more harshly than the method most common among whites. Based on the racial and socioeconomic differences among those prosecuted for crack and powder cocaine offenses (since crack is less expensive, its use is more widespread among less affluent people than powder cocaine), groups such as the American Civil Liberties Union and Families Against Mandatory Minimums have issued statements urging the Federal Sentencing Commission to reconsider these sentencing guidelines. Although the disparities have been successfully challenged in some state and district courts, the U.S. Department of Justice stated in 1995 that it would reject any proposal to equate the two forms of the drug, claiming that crack is more dangerous and harmful than powder cocaine.

COCAINE AND THE INNER CITY

Through the 1970s and early 1980s, use of cocaine was not yet epidemic in the inner cities. The high price of cocaine powder meant

A mural makes the point that drugs do nothing to enhance life. Many of the efforts to keep young people off drugs focus on promoting the image of drugs as "uncool."

that using the drug was unfeasible for the inner cities' residents, most of whom were of lower socioeconomic classes than residents of the suburbs. In the mid-1980s, when crack cocaine appeared, its use began to spread to the inner cities, encouraged by the lower prices and the fact that crack was typically sold in smaller amounts—often in single doses.

While powder cocaine was most frequently sold in wholesale quantities behind closed doors, crack dealers set up open-air "markets," offering their wares to passersby. As a result of their presence, and the violence associated with their trade, violent crime rates in inner-city

DRUG DEALING NOT A LUCRATIVE BUSINESS

Television shows and movies often portray drug dealers as rich and powerful, driving luxury automobiles and wearing lots of gold jewelry. But dealing drugs is not an easy way to get rich; in fact, a drug dealer looking for customers outside the local fast-food restaurant may make less than the person flipping burgers inside.

A study by economist Steven Levitt of the University of Chicago and sociologist Sudhir Venkatesh of Harvard University found that the bottom-level dealers make just $3 an hour. The only ones who make money on drugs are the gang leaders, who can make as much as $65 an hour while confining the risks—arrest, murder by a rival gang member—to the low-level pushers. But because of poverty in the inner cities, there are always youths attracted by the glamour of gangs and drugs that are willing to fill these dealer positions.

"There's the mythology that the media has built about the lucrativeness of pushing drugs, but the lessons of introductory economics suggest it can't be true," Levitt told *Forbes* magazine in August 1998. "These are kids with very low skills and there's a reserve army of them waiting to get into the gang. Competition would suggest that the employer [the gang leader] has all the power in this relationship."

Most youths join a gang in hopes of rising to the top of the power structure, and thus achieving the power and money that come with being leader of the gang. However, in the violent world of drug gangs, few ever reach that level. "Right now, the kids are completely getting the calculation wrong about what the likelihood is they're going to rise up in the gang," Venkatesh told *Forbes*. Educating gang members about the drug "business" may lead some of them to take legitimate jobs or inspire them to remain in school and get an education.

neighborhoods began to rise. "Crack houses" where the drug was sold and smoked proliferated as dealers took over abandoned buildings.

In addition to the health and social problems caused by the crack use itself, many inner-city neighborhoods saw their rates of HIV infection rise as a result of the drug's influence. A study done in 1994 of inner-city residents in Miami, New York, and San Francisco found that people who smoked crack were 2.4 times more likely to be infected with HIV than nonsmokers. In New York and Miami, approximately 30 percent of women who had sex in exchange for drugs or money were HIV-infected. The high-risk sexual behaviors of the crack-smoking group seemed to have caused this high rate of infection, researchers concluded.

The news is not all bad, however. A study of trends in drug-related arrests in New York showed that cocaine arrests (most of which involve crack cocaine) had dropped from 54,000 in 1989 down to 38,000 in 1991—a decline of around 30 percent. Births to crack- or cocaine-addicted women appeared to be decreasing at about the same rate, from 3,200 in 1989 to 2,200 in 1991. In Washington, D.C., the number of adult arrestees who tested positive for cocaine use dropped by close to 20 percent between 1988 and 1993. A large part of this effect seems to be due to the growing perception of crack cocaine users as "neighborhood burnouts," as reported in the winter 1997 edition of *Pulse Check*. Apparently, seeing how crack addicts are affected by the drug has convinced many young people not to use it themselves.

COCAINE AND YOUNG ADULTS

The NIDA published a study in 1995 called *Monitoring the Future*, which took survey data from high school students every year for 20 years to try to determine the trends in drug use among American youth. The results of the study, covering the years from 1975 to 1995, show some positive results: cocaine use has remained low, and a high percentage of high school students say they disapprove of cocaine use.

Cocaine use in the period of the study peaked in 1986, the same year crack first showed up in survey questions. The number of high school seniors saying that they had used cocaine in the previous year hit a high of about 13 percent that year. After that peak, use declined rapidly, falling to a level of about 3 percent by 1991 and remaining steady at about 3 or 4 percent for the next four years. Crack use, which was tracked as a separate problem, also peaked in 1986, with just under 5 percent of seniors reporting use in the previous year, and has since fallen to a level of about 2 or 2.5 percent.

One possible cause for this decline is the increasing number of students who perceive cocaine use to be a "great risk." About 87 percent of students responded in 1995 that they associated regular use of cocaine with "great risk," up from 72 percent 20 years earlier. The numbers for crack are slightly higher, with 90 percent perceiving "great risk" for regular use, up from 80 percent the first year crack was surveyed. In both cases more than half of students believe there is a "great risk" involved in trying cocaine or crack even once or twice. The figures for disapproval are even higher: 90 percent of high school seniors reported that they disapproved of using crack or cocaine even once or twice. The combination of these factors— perceived risk and disapproval—may help to explain why cocaine use among young people has fallen even though its availability is still relatively high (almost half of high school seniors reported that cocaine was fairly easy or very easy to get). The data seem to show that more young people are aware of the dangers of drug use than they have been previously and that their increasing awareness is helping them choose not to use cocaine.

■   ■   ■

As this book shows, cocaine abuse can seriously affect a person's life, causing problems in school or on the job, deterioration of relationships with family or friends, and serious health problems. Cocaine can even lead to death, as the stories of John Belushi, Len Bias, and others in this book suggest. Unfortunately, the problem of drug abuse continues to grow. From 1992 to 1998, drug use rates nearly doubled.

In 1997 the U.S. Congress appropriated $195 million for a new series of television, radio, newspaper, and magazine advertisements designed to educate children and teens about the negative effects of drug use. As with Nancy Reagan's "Just Say No" campaign during the 1980s, Drug Czar Barry McCaffrey hopes that this new advertising/ education campaign, called the "National Youth Anti-Drug Media Campaign," will reduce the rising number of young adults who use illegal substances. Experts at the National Office of Drug Control Policy hope that this campaign will began to influence teens' attitudes toward drugs within two years.

But while it is essential that lawmakers, teachers, and counselors continue to wage war on illegal drugs, parents are the most important part of drug prevention. Positive parental involvement in children's' lives and family efforts to educate children about the dangers of cocaine will be the best way to reduce drug use by the next generation.

APPENDIX

FOR MORE INFORMATION

The following are good sources for information on and help overcoming cocaine and crack abuse.

American Council for Drug Education
164 West 74th Street
New York, NY 10023
(212) 758-8060
1-800-448-DRUG

Cocaine Anonymous
3740 Overland Avenue, Suite G
Los Angeles, CA 90034
(213) 559-5833
1-800-347-8988

CoAnon Family Groups
P.O. Box 64742-66
Los Angeles, CA 90064
(310) 859-2206

Hazelden Foundation/Pleasant Valley Road
P.O. Box 176
Center City, MN 55012
1-800-328-9000

Nar-Anon Family Groups
P.O. Box 2562
Palos Verdes Peninsula, CA 90274
(310) 547-5800

Narcotics Anonymous
P.O. Box 9999
Van Nuys, CA 91409
(818) 780-3951

National Clearinghouse for Alcohol and Drug Information
P.O. Box 2345
Rockville, MD 20847-2345
(301) 468-2600
1-800-729-6686

National Council on Alcoholism and Drug Dependence
12 West 21st Street, 7th Floor
New York, NY 10010
1-800-622-2255

National Families in Action
2296 Henderson Mill Road, Suite 300
Atlanta, GA 30345
(404) 934-6364

Center for Substance Abuse Treatment
Information and Treatment Referral
    Hotline
11426-28 Rockville Pike, Suite 410
Rockville, MD 20852
1-800-662-HELP

There are also drug treatment programs and information hot lines listed in the telephone directories of almost every city. Many hospitals and medical centers sponsor drug programs as well. Schools, colleges, and drug prevention projects are also good sources for information.

APPENDIX

STATISTICS

TABLE 1: DRUG USER EXPENDITURES (in billions of dollars)

Drug	1988	1989	1990	1991	1992	1993	1994	1995
Cocaine	61.2	56.7	51.5	45.9	41.7	40.3	37.4	38.0
Heroin	17.7	16.8	14.3	11.9	10.2	9.8	9.3	9.6
Marijuana	9.1	10.9	11.0	10.7	11.5	8.8	8.2	7.0
Other	3.3	2.8	2.2	2.3	2.0	1.5	2.6	2.7
Totals	**91.4**	**87.2**	**79.0**	**70.7**	**65.4**	**60.4**	**57.5**	**57.3**

Note: Amounts are in constant 1996 dollars.
Source: Abt Associates, Inc., *What America's Users Spend on Illegal Drugs: 1988-1995* (November 1997).

TABLE 2: ESTIMATED NUMBER OF HARD-CORE AND OCCASIONAL USERS OF COCAINE AND HEROIN (Thousands), 1988-1995

Use	1988	1989	1990	1991	1992	1993	1994	1995
Cocaine								
Casual users (use less often than weekly)	6039	5313	4587	4478	3503	3332	2930	3082
Heavy users (use at least weekly)	4140	3889	3674	3501	3528	3598	3610	3620
Heroin								
Casual users (use less often than weekly)	167	152	136	172	207	199	206	322
Heavy users	876	881	784	730	692	787	799	810

Note: Data in this table are preliminary composite estimates from the National Household Survey on Drug Abuse (NHSDA) and the Drug Use Forecasting (DUF) program. The NHSDA was not administered in 1989. Estimates for 1989 are the average for 1988 and 1989.
Source: Abt Associates, Inc., *What America's Users Spend on Illicit Drugs: 1988-1995* (November 1997).

TABLE 3: PREVALENCE OF DRUG USE (%) AMONG 6th-8th, 9th-12th, and 12th GRADE STUDENTS, 1994-95, 1995-96, and 1996-97

Annual Use	1994-95	1995-96	1996-97	Change*	Monthly Use	1994-95	1995-96	1996-97	Change*
Cigarettes					**Cigarettes**				
6th-8th	28.1	31.1	31.8	+0.7 s	6th-8th	15.7	17.2	17.3	+0.1
9th-12th	44.4	48.2	50.2	+2.0 s	9th-12th	31.3	33.4	34.7	+1.3 s
12th	46.8	50.0	52.4	+2.4 s	12th	34.6	36.2	38.3	+2.1 s
Beer					**Beer**				
6th-8th	30.8	33.1	33.2	+0.1	6th-8th	11.8	12.5	12.1	-0.4 s
9th-12th	57.4	59.1	59.6	+0.5 s	9th-12th	33.3	34.3	34.4	+0.1
12th	64.0	64.9	65.3	+0.4	12th	40.6	41.2	41.7	+0.5
Wine Coolers					**Wine Coolers**				
6th-8th	29.8	33.2	33.6	+0.4	6th-8th	9.8	10.8	10.8	+0.0
9th-12th	51.7	52.6	52.9	+0.3	9th-12th	23.1	22.3	22.3	+0.0
12th	56.5	54.5	55.4	+0.9	12th	25.6	22.9	23.7	+0.8
Liquor					**Liquor**				
6th-8th	21.3	22.9	23.7	+0.8 s	6th-8th	8.5	9.0	9.1	+0.1
9th-12th	51.5	53.4	54.9	+1.5 s	9th-12th	27.4	28.2	28.7	+0.5 s
12th	59.5	59.9	62.3	+2.4 s	12th	32.5	32.8	34.0	+1.2 s
Marijuana					**Marijuana**				
6th-8th	9.5	13.6	14.7	+1.1 s	6th-8th	5.7	8.1	8.6	+0.5 s
9th-12th	28.2	34.0	35.8	+1.8 s	9th-12th	18.5	22.3	22.7	+0.4
12th	33.2	37.9	39.4	+1.5 s	12th	20.9	24.3	24.4	+0.1
Cocaine					**Cocaine**				
6th-8th	1.9	2.7	3.0	+0.3 s	6th-8th	1.2	1.5	1.7	+0.2 s
9th-12th	4.5	5.6	5.9	+0.3 s	9th-12th	2.6	2.9	3.0	+0.1
12th	5.3	7.1	7.0	-0.1	12th	2.9	3.6	3.6	+0.0
Uppers					**Uppers**				
6th-8th	3.3	4.6	4.9	+0.3 s	6th-8th	2.0	2.4	2.6	+0.2 s
9th-12th	9.3	10.5	10.3	-0.2	9th-12th	5.1	5.2	5.3	+0.1
12th	10.6	11.6	10.7	-0.9 s	12th	5.6	5.8	5.6	-0.2
Downers					**Downers**				
6th-8th	2.4	3.5	4.0	+0.5 s	6th-8th	1.5	1.9	2.1	+0.2 s
9th-12th	5.5	7.1	7.2	+0.1	9th-12th	3.4	3.8	3.8	+0.0
12th	5.9	7.4	7.4	+0.0	12th	3.6	4.1	3.9	-0.2
Inhalants					**Inhalants**				
6th-8th	6.3	8.5	8.9	+0.4 s	6th-8th	2.9	3.5	3.7	+0.2
9th-12th	7.5	7.6	7.1	-0.5 s	9th-12th	3.5	3.4	3.1	-0.3 s
12th	6.6	6.6	5.8	-0.8 s	12th	3.0	3.1	2.7	-0.4 s
Hallucinogens					**Hallucinogens**				
6th-8th	2.4	3.3	3.6	+0.3 s	6th-8th	1.5	1.8	2.0	+0.2 s
9th-12th	7.7	9.5	9.5	+0.0	9th-12th	4.1	4.5	4.2	-0.3 s
12th	9.7	12.1	11.7	-0.4	12th	4.8	5.1	4.6	-0.5

* Note: Level of significance of difference between the 1995-96 and 1996-97 surveys: s=0.05, using chi-square with variables year and use/no use.

SAMPLE SIZES:	Grade	1994-95	1995-96	1996-97
	6th-8th	92,453	58,596	68,071
	9th-12th	105,788	70,964	73,006
	12th	20,698	14,261	15,532

Source: PRIDE USA Survey 1994–95, 1995–96, and 1996–97.

TABLE 4: PERCENTAGE REPORTING COCAINE USE IN THEIR LIFETIME, BY AGE GROUP AND DEMOGRAPHIC CHARACTERISTICS: 1995

Demographic Characteristic	Age Group (Years) 12-17	18-25	26-34	35+	Total
Total	2.0	9.8	21.6	8.6	10.3
Gender					
Male	2.0	10.5	24.3	12.0	12.8
Female	2.0	9.1	18.9	5.6	7.9
Race/Ethnicity[1]					
White	2.3	11.8	25.5	8.9	11.3
Black	0.4	2.1	11.9	10.6	8.1
Hispanic	2.0	7.6	14.8	5.7	7.5
Population Density					
Large Metro	1.8	9.6	20.8	10.0	11.2
Small Metro	2.2	10.6	25.6	8.1	10.7
Nonmetro	2.1	8.8	17.3	6.7	8.0
Region					
Northeast	0.9	11.9	22.4	9.5	11.2
North Central	2.4	8.9	19.8	7.0	8.9
South	1.5	7.6	19.2	6.7	8.3
West	3.1	12.0	25.8	12.7	13.9
Adult Education[2]					
Less than high school	N/A	13.4	25.8	3.7	8.5
High school graduate	N/A	11.6	22.4	9.3	12.0
Some college	N/A	7.3	21.8	11.0	12.4
College graduate	N/A	5.9	18.1	9.6	11.1
Current Employment[3]					
Full-time	N/A	11.0	21.6	12.3	14.4
Part-time	N/A	8.0	23.7	8.7	11.1
Unemployed	N/A	13.0	26.8	19.8	19.6
Other[4]	N/A	7.7	17.9	3.0	4.8

N/A: Not applicable

Note: Due to improved procedures implemented in 1994, these estimates are not comparable to those presented in NHSDA Main Findings prior to 1994.

[1] The category "other" for Race/Ethnicity is not included.

[2] Data on adult education are not applicable for youth age 12-17. Total refers to adults age 18 and older (unweighted N=13, 152).

[3] Data on current employment are not applicable for youth age 12-17. Total refers to adults age 18 and older (unweighted N=13, 152).

[4] Retired, disabled, homemaker, student, or "other."

Source: Office of Applied Studies, SAMHSA, National Household Survey on Drug Abuse, 1995.

APPENDIX

GLOSSARY

Attention-deficit/hyperactivity disorder: A psychological disorder in which the person is unable to concentrate on tasks or becomes hyperactive. Cocaine use can compound this disorder.

Binge: an extreme period of cocaine use that typically lasts several days. Binges are often associated with cocaine dependence, usually end only when the supply of cocaine is exhausted, and are often followed by an intense period of withdrawal, called a "crash."

Cocaine: the psychoactive component of the coca plant, *Erythroxylon coca.* Cocaine's most common form is as a white powder that can be inhaled ("snorted") or injected intravenously.

Crack: A solid, inexpensive form of cocaine formed by mixing cocaine, hydrochloride salt, and baking soda, then allowing the mixture to dry into nuggets called "rocks." The drug is usually smoked.

Delirium: a disturbance of consciousness and the thought process, characterized by an inability to focus, sustain, or shift attention; ease of distraction by irrelevant stimuli; and reduced clarity of awareness of the environment.

Detoxification: the physical process in which a person's body rids itself of drugs. Also, any treatment program designed to help a person do so.

Freebase: The cocaine base that occurs when the hydrochloride is removed from cocaine hydrochloride. "Freebasing" is a term for the process by which this base is made. Freebase cocaine is commonly smoked, and delivers a more intense high than snorting cocaine.

Intoxication: the changes in a person's physical or mental state brought on by the presence of cocaine. The most common effects of cocaine intoxication include difficulties in perception, a feeling of wakefulness or heightened awareness, impairment to attention span and judgment, disruptive behavior, and awkward physical movement.

Mood disorders: a group of psychological disorders, including depression and manic depression, characterized by extreme mood swings that impair a person's ability to function normally in society and that can, in severe cases, drive someone to attempt suicide. Cocaine use may exacerbate previously unnoticed mood disorder symptoms.

Neurotransmitters: chemicals that allow the brain and central nervous system to communicate by passing electrical impulses back and forth, allowing the body to feel and respond to pleasure or pain. Cocaine blocks certain neurotransmitters, such as norepinephrine, dopamine, and serotonin. This causes the drug's stimulating effects, but in high doses it can lead to convulsions, coma, or death.

Physical dependence: When a drug user's body has become so used to the substance that unpleasant physical symptoms will occur if he or she stops taking the drug.

Psychological dependence: The drug user has a powerful craving to use the drug, even if there is no physical need to do so (see Physical dependence).

Substance-induced disorders: mental problems, such as mood disorders, delirium, or a psychotic disorder, that are caused by the use of drugs.

Substance-use disorders: using a drug in an unhealthy manner, or the effects of doing so. Cocaine dependence and cocaine abuse are classified as substance-use disorders by the American Psychiatric Association.

Therapeutic community: a treatment option originally developed for heroin users but now common to multidrug and adolescent drug addicts, in which patients live in a structured, drug-free environment where they receive therapy and learn how to socialize and have productive lives without using drugs.

Tolerance: the addict's need for increasing amounts of a drug to achieve the same level of intoxication. Long-term addicts may develop such high tolerance that they can take amounts that would kill a nonuser.

Withdrawal: the physical and mental symptoms that occur when a person who is physically dependent on a drug stops taking the drug. Withdrawal symptoms have been likened to a bad case of the flu, with muscle aches and cramps, fever, vomiting, and weakness, as well as mental symptoms such as depression and hallucinations.

APPENDIX

BIBLIOGRAPHY

Alcohol, Drug Abuse, and Mental Health Administration. *Cocaine/Crack: The Big Lie.* Washington, D.C.: U.S. Government Printing Office, 1991.

American Council for Drug Education. "Cocaine, Crack, Crank and Ice" (pamphlet). Rockville, M.D.: ACDE Press, 1990.

Booth, Cathy. "Caribbean Blizzard: With Blissful Vacationers Unaware, Tons of Cocaine Flow Through the Idyllic Islands, Thanks to Sharkish Drug Cartels." *Time* 147, no. 9 (February 26, 1996).

Edlin, Brian R., Kathleen L. Irwin, Sarius Faruque, et al. "Intersecting Epidemics—Crack Cocaine Use and HIV Infection Among Inner-City Young Adults." *New England Journal of Medicine* 331, no. 21 (November 1994).

Elber, Lynn. "Movies Don't Mix Drugs, Glamor, Despite Dole Attacks." *The Salt Lake Tribune,* November 1, 1996.

Gavzer, Bernard. "Can They Beat the Odds?" *Parade Magazine,* July 27, 1997.

Gawin, F. H., and E. H. Ellinwood. "Cocaine and other Stimulants: Actions, Abuse, and Treatment." *New England Journal of Medicine* 318 (1988).

Gladwell, Malcom, "New York Crack Epidemic Appears to Wane: Seeing Drug's Destructiveness, Younger People Are Turning Away." *Washington Post,* May 31, 1993.

Harrison, Keith, and Sally Jenkins. "Maryland Basketball Star Len Bias is Dead at 22." *The Washington Post,* June 20, 1986.

Holden, Constance. "Street-Wise Crack Research." *Science,* December 15, 1989.

Johanson, Chris-Ellyn. *Cocaine: A New Epidemic.* New York: Chelsea House Publishers, 1992.

LaFraniere, Sharon. "Barry Arrested on Cocaine Charges in Undercover FBI, Police Operation." *Washington Post,* January 19, 1990.

Massing, Michael. "Crack's Destructive Sprint Across America." *New York Times Magazine,* October 1, 1989.

National Clearinghouse for Alcohol and Drug Abuse. *Tips for Teens About Crack and Cocaine*. Available at: http://www.health.org/pubs/tips/teen-coke.html

National Families in Action. *Drug Info: Cocaine Fact Sheet*. Available at: http://www.lec.org/DrugSearch/Documents/Cocaine.html

————. *Drug Info: Crack Fact Sheet*. Available at: http://www.lec.org/DrugSearch/Documents/Crack.html

Office of National Drug Control Policy. *The National Drug Control Strategy, 1998: A Ten Year Plan*. Washington, D.C.: U.S. Government Printing Office, 1998.

————. *What America's Users Spend on Illegal Drugs, 1988-1995*. Washington, D.C.: U.S. Government Printing Office, 1997.

————. *Pulse Check: National Trends in Drug Abuse (Winter 1997)*. Washington, D.C.: U.S. Government Printing Office, 1997.

PennSAIC. "About Cocaine and Pregnancy" (pamphlet). Deerfield, Mass.: Channing L. Bete Co., 1993.

————. "Cocaine." (pamphlet). Deerfield, Mass.: Channing L. Bete Co., 1993.

————. "Cocaine." (pamphlet). Northfield, Minn: Life Skills Education, 1992.

————. "Turn Your Back on Crack!" (pamphlet). Deerfield, Mass.: Channing L. Bete Co., 1996.

RxList Generic Information. *Cocaine*. Available at: http://www.rxlist.com/cgi/generic/cocaine.html

U.S. Department of Justice. *Drugs, Crime, and the Justice System*. Washington, D.C.: U.S. Government Printing Office, 1992.

Woolley, Scott. "Greedy Bosses: Running Drugs Isn't as Lucrative as it May Seem." *Forbes* 162, no. 4 (August 24, 1998).

APPENDIX

FURTHER READING

American Psychiatric Association. *Diagnostic and Statistical Manual of Mental Disorders*, 4th edition. Washington, D.C.: American Psychiatric Press, 1994.

———. *Treatment of Psychiatric Disorders*, 2nd edition. 2 vols. Washington, D.C.: American Psychiatric Press, 1994.

Chier, Ruth. *Danger: Cocaine.* New York: Powerkids Press, 1997.

Eddy, Paul. *The Cocaine Wars.* New York: Norton, 1988.

Erickson, Patricia, et al. *The Steel Drug: Cocaine in Perspective.* Lexington, Mass.: Lexington Books, 1986.

Faude, Jeffrey, and Mark David. *Psychotherapy of Cocaine Addiction: Entering the Interpersonal World of the Cocaine Addict.* New York: Jason Aronson, 1997.

Johanson, Chris-Ellyn. *Cocaine: A New Epidemic.* New York: Chelsea House Publishers, 1992.

Karch, Steven B. *A Brief History of Cocaine.* Grand Rapids, Mich.: CRC Publications, 1997.

Kendall, Sarita H. *Cocaine: The Complete Story.* Austin, Texas: Steck-Vaughn, 1992.

McFarland, Rhoda. *Cocaine.* New York: Rosen Publishing Group, 1997.

Mermelstein, Max. *Inside the Cocaine Cartel: The Riveting Eyewitness Account of Life Inside the Colombian Cartel.* Bedford, N.H.: Spi Books, 1993.

Morales, Edmundo. *Cocaine: White Gold Rush in Peru.* Tucson: University of Arizona Press, 1989.

Platt, Jerome J. *Cocaine Addiction: Theory, Research, and Treatment.* Cambridge, Mass.: Harvard University Press, 1997.

Rivers, James, Dale D. Chitwood, and James A. Inciardi. *The American Pipe Dream, Crack Cocaine and the Inner City.* Fort Worth, Texas: Harcourt Brace College Publishers, 1995.

Scott, Peter Dale, and Jonathan Marshall. *Cocaine Politics: Drugs, Armies, and the CIA in Central America.* Berkeley, Calif.: University of California Press, 1998.

Shaffer, Howard J., and Stephanie B. Jones. *Cocaine: The Struggle Against Impulse.* Lexington, Mass.: Lexington Books, 1988.

Williams, Terry. *The Cocaine Kids: The Inside Story of a Teenage Drug Ring.* Reading, Mass.: Addison-Wesley, 1989.

APPENDIX

INDEX

APPENDIX

PICTURE CREDITS

8: Courtesy Drug Enforcement Agency
10: AP/Wide World Photos
13: AP/Wide World Photos
15: AP/Wide World Photos
17: Courtesy Drug Enforcement Agency
18: AP/Wide World Photos
19: UPI/Corbis-Bettmann
22: Courtesy Drug Enforcement Agency
24: Courtesy National Library of Medicine
27: AP/Wide World Photos
30: AP/Wide World Photos; inset: AP/Wide World Photos
32: Lawrence Migdale/Photo Researchers, Inc.
35: Globe Photos, Inc.
38: Arthur Tress/Photo Researchers, Inc.
40: Bob Combs/Photo Researchers, Inc.

43: AP/Wide World Photos
44: UPI/Corbis-Bettmann
46: AP/Wide World Photos
50: UPI/Corbis-Bettmann
53: Jan Halaska/Photo Researchers, Inc.
57: Oscar Burriel/Photo Researchers, Inc.
58: Rouchon/Photo Researchers, Inc.
60: Jeff Greenberg/Photo Researchers, Inc.
62: UPI/Corbis-Bettmann
65: UPI/Corbis-Bettmann
67: AP/Wide World Photos
69: AP/Wide World Photos
70: Courtesy National Library of Medicine
73: AP/Wide World Photos
75: Courtesy Drug Enforcement Agency
77: Courtesy The United Nations

Senior Consulting Editor Carol C. Nadelson, M.D., is president and chief executive officer of the American Psychiatric Press, Inc., staff physician at Cambridge Hospital, and Clinical Professor of Psychiatry at Harvard Medical School. In addition to her work with the American Psychiatric Association, which she served as vice president in 1981-83 and president in 1985-86, Dr. Nadelson has been actively involved in other major psychiatric organizations, including the Group for the Advancement of Psychiatry, the American College of Psychiatrists, the Association for Academic Psychiatry, the American Association of Directors of Psychiatric Residency Training Programs, the American Psychosomatic Society, and the American College of Mental Health Administrators. In addition, she has been a consultant to the Psychiatric Education Branch of the National Institute of Mental Health and has served on the editorial boards of several journals. Doctor Nadelson has received many awards, including the Gold Medal Award for significant and ongoing contributions in the field of psychiatry, the Elizabeth Blackwell Award for contributions to the causes of women in medicine, and the Distinguished Service Award from the American College of Psychiatrists for outstanding achievements and leadership in the field of psychiatry.

Consulting Editor Claire E. Reinburg, M.A., is editorial director of the American Psychiatric Press, Inc., which publishes about 60 new books and six journals a year. She is a graduate of Georgetown University in Washington, D.C., where she earned bachelor of arts and master of arts degrees in English. She is a member of the Council of Biology Editors, the Women's National Book Association, the Society for Scholarly Publishing, and Washington Book Publishers.

Ann Holmes has written and edited professionally for over 15 years. Her special areas of interest are both cultural and medical topics. Her books include *The Mental Effects of Heroin* in Chelsea House Publishers' Encyclopedia of Psychological Disorders. Ann and her family live in southwestern Pennsylvania, where she edits *The Loyalhanna Review*, the literary journal of the Ligonier Valley Writers.